SOUL CODE

Near-death experiences, pre-birth memories, between-lives regressions, induced after-death communications, transformative occurrences and what they tell us about who we really are.

By
Matthew DeBow

Dedicated To
My son, Luca, and his spiritual path on this wondrous planet.

**We are not human beings having a spiritual experience.
We are spiritual beings having a human experience.**
Pierre Tielhard de Chardin

CREDITS

Editors
Dan Terry & Patricia Marquez

Development & Editorial Assistance
Shane Matthews, Patsy Shepard, Elizabeth Hethera,
Ryan Janik, Cheryl Mackin & Coy Matula

Formatting & Editorial Review
Dan Terry

Photo Credit
Brian Hulbert & Sandra DeBow

Editorial Consulting
Jonathan De la Luz

Special Thanks
Manuel Inverno

Thanks To
The people who have come forth with their transformation experiences, and all of the people that graciously allowed me to interview them about it. The people that dedicate careers and personal time to hospice. Appreciation to the International Association of Near Death Studies.

Special Mention
Edward Salisbury, Michael Shuster, Joe Fisher & Walter Makichen

SOUL CODE

Table of Contents

FOREWORD
Dan Terry

The soul has a code. Like our bodies have a code in DNA that defines and shapes our package and perception of existence, DeBow explores and introduces a lexicon of understanding into the hidden messages that emerge in specifically human experience and phenomena that is soul speak into truths beyond our current ability to quantify, prove, fully comprehend, and measure.

DeBow has done the world a noble service in pouring over volumes of data, picking through countless studies, and compiling extensive interviews to present this macro view across a broad spectrum of scientific, medical, biological, spiritual and religious disciplines to produce a fascinating collection of evidence that points to a clearer vision of the concept of soul itself and our role in the bigger game of existence, in and beyond biological life and human consciousness.

Beyond that, by conglomerating and comparing the diversity of explorations and studies into matters that confront science, medicine and religious beliefs that overlap into the realms of spirituality or the paranormal, DeBow has compiled a lexicon for mutual understanding by recognizing common root symbols of a language of spirituality and religion and science and psychology that today uses different terms all meaning the same thing. He helps us understand the commonalities in various disciplines that are part of the soul's code trying to emerge into human consciousness.

As Jung pioneered an understanding of the subconscious's dream imagery as a symbolic visual language, DeBow is pioneering a similar understanding of the soul's language as reported by NDE's and others describing spiritual and mystical events. What most describe is beyond common earthy experience and in reporting the incomprehensible is filtered through a language limited to things known and within the bounds of imagination. Psychologists report it filtered through their jargon, priests through the language of Biblical texts, children with the limited vocabulary of their age. The souls or Universe's language is tinted a thousand different shades, all a pale hint of its actual truth as it's diluted through the various lexicons of philosophical or professional shop talk.

What is clear is that for the vast majority of persons on the planet, our language and conscious experience is nearly infinitely too limited to express or fully comprehend. Like Jung's dream imagery are symbolic allegories into the subconscious's concept of reality, in the realms of those exploring and researching the soul or spirits journey, the words describing realms beyond physical human experience are mere allegorical symbols offering no more than a tiny glimpse of the whole. DeBow offers the first comprehensive macro level glimpse of a range of those symbols and experiences as reported across scientific, research, religious and paranormal disciples. In so doing we can begin to see and comprehend the universal truths, glimpsed in part, by many, and described and shared in languages exclusively by words, inherently limited, which in the aggregate paint a clearer symbolic vision of the realms of the soul.

As the artists of classic times identified, defined and categorized the language of perspective to better express and depict the 3-dimensional world on two dimensional canvases, today's researchers into the soul realm, are creating such a language that collectively translates dimensions and consciousness beyond physical experience into our limited 3D perception. What is clear when seen as DeBow presents it, is regardless of perceptual framework shaped by profession, belief, or life experience, the realm of the soul and it's reality remains infinitely beyond our ability to reduce it to fit into our human sensory experience and comprehension. Except symbolically.

Though the words, terms and even meanings differ across disciplines and beliefs, what emerges when compared and contrasted, is a symbolic lexicon that frames the infinite such that we can wrap our minds around it, if only to begin fathoming the truth of the soul's mysteries.

INTRODUCTION

"In a gentle way you can shake the world."
Mahatma Gandhi

My curiosity and interest in metaphysics started very young. I remember having bizarre episodes (usually at night) when time appeared to speed up and motion appeared to increase in velocity. I would start crying, and it made my mother upset because she felt powerless to help me. It was as if time had stretched onward, and like a rubber band was bouncing back.

Even though these occurrences were infrequent and rarely lasted long, my parents were concerned enough about the incidents to arrange an electroencephalography (EEG) examination at San Francisco State University Hospital. Strangely enough, when I was placed in front of the brainwave analysis equipment. Very advanced technology at the time, my first thought was that the equipment looked old and antiquated. I was six years old and had never seen anything like it before. So, why should I have thought this?

Other strange things occurred in my childhood. When I held batteries, a strange acidic taste would come into my mouth. In kindergarten, I noticed that while looking at the teacher during the lessons in class her face would appear to be closer than it actually was. This only seemed to happen when I gazed into an intense stare.

Even at such a young age, these experiences set me to thinking about the complexities of the brain and how it worked. I began to wonder how it was possible that everything appeared to speed up for me, while everyone else perceived life continuing along at a normal, regular pace.

**"Imagination is more important
than knowledge."**
Albert Einstein

There were other incidents of a slightly different, albeit still strange nature. Once, as a child, I saw what I would call a "ghostly apparition" that had a keen interest in a group of us children. It resembled a pale, whitish semi-transparent plasma energy. From my perspective it was able to hide behind poles and objects much thinner and smaller than its original size and appearance. When turning my attention towards it, it would recognize me; that I had seen it and had attempted to quickly dodge my awareness of it. It was not successful.

Another time, I spent the night at the house of my friend and neighbor, Mike Cummins. I was awakened in the middle of the night by Mike's two dogs, Snoopy and Duchess, outside and very excited about something. I went to the window and saw what appeared to be elves or fairies running and playing among the dogs. Fearful of being seen by them, I ran quickly back to the sleeping bags where Mike and his brother, Dave, had been sleeping. I tried to wake Mike, shaking him and saying his name, but he wouldn't wake up; he was clearly in a bizarre, deep sleep. Dave was older, and the neighborhood bully, so I knew better than to try to wake him up. Was this a dream? To this day, I cannot say.

My family went on many trips with another family, the Wirts, who had kids of similar ages. They had moved to a new subdivision on the outskirts of Sacramento, California. One warm summer night, we kids decided to camp out in the back yard. Later, as we were messing around, one of the kids pointed out a strange light far off in the distance. This bright pinpoint of light appeared to be slowly moving across the horizon, back and forth, making no noise. One of the older kids called it UFO, that was the first time I had ever heard that term.

Occurrences like these—primarily my sense that time behaved differently for me—catapulted me into reading about extra-sensory perception (ESP), the paranormal, and other mysteries. As a fifth grader, the book I chose for one of my class assignments was *The Reincarnation of Peter Proud*. The teacher's surprise was clearly evident.

Years later I mentioned to my father my interest in these topics. I was surprised to learn that there was a period in his young life when he too was quite curious about paranormal matters and also read books about ESP. But I did not find out until much later that there had been an influencing factor in this interest that he had failed to mention.

> **"Our spiritual attitude is determined by our conception of our relation to infinite spirit."**
> *Paul Twitchell*

Allow me to explain. My grandfather on my dad's side died several years before I was born, and my grandmother married a man named Spate. So I had always known her as "Grandma Spate." One day, I was renting a mini-storage unit in Chico, California, and the woman working there saw my last name when I was filling out the paperwork. She said that she used to know a card reader named DeBow. I asked, "What do you mean? A card reader?" She explained how this woman could read regular playing cards and tell you your future. Then she said the woman had lived in Oakland, California, which was where my dad grew up and I was born.

My grandmother was still alive then, so the next time I saw her I asked, "Do you know of a mystic card reader with the last name De-Bow?" It took her a minute to respond, her eyes widening in surprise. "Yes, that was me!" And she proceeded to tell me how, when she was still Mrs. DeBow, she used to read regular playing cards to raise money for charities. At first, it was only for fun, but eventually, she became very good at it. However, there was one time, she explained, her voice becoming quiet, when she read a woman's cards and the layout foretold that someone she knew was going to die. My grandmother was surprised by the reading, but was even more shocked when, the next day, the woman's husband died! My grandmother resolved never to read cards again.

Therefore it seems my interest was not out-of-place—metaphysical and spiritual phenomena have interested my family for generations, and my interest has persisted to this day.

Needless to say, while growing up, I wanted to better understand these mysterious matters. I wanted to get to the core of these strange occurrences, but I wanted to do this in a scientific, quantifiable way. So, of course, I continued my reading and expanded my studies into several areas of esoteric knowledge.

However, I found that, over time, as much as I tried to avoid looking into conventional religion to find the answers, I discovered bits and pieces clearly connecting religion and philosophy to the information I sought. What I also realized is that words and concepts such as "soul," "heaven," "god," and "eternity" are not only an integral part of nearly all religions, but are also integral to spiritual and esoteric information. I began to wonder if these words were a part of the first theosophical language of the heavens.

> **"Each soul enters with a mission.**
> **We all have a mission to perform."**
> *Edgar Cayce*

It became clear that, no matter what culture we are born into, the quest for truth and wisdom is always present within man. In Western cultures, the first stories of paranormal and/or miraculous events come from biblical stories, fairy tales, and Norse, Celtic, Greek, and Roman mythology. In nearly all other cultures, there are similar stories that have been passed down from generations of elders and mystics. Moreover, in today's media-saturated society, all of us, especially children, are inundated with notions of paranormal experiences from Hollywood television and film projects. Therefore, it should be each person's personal prerogative to seek a heightened understanding. There are abundant opportunities to explore that which is profound, and, if we let it guide us, our journeys lead each of us toward an insightful and spiritual path.

Nevertheless, until a few years ago, in spite of all the books I read and other information I had uncovered, I found that I still hadn't acquired the answers I was looking for. Until, at one point during my quest, I began to read reports about people coming back from the brink of death.

With technological advancements in medical resuscitation procedures, people began coming back to life after having being dead, in extreme cases, for over fifteen minutes. And many of those who were revived came back with incredible tales of being out of the body, visiting an amazingly beautiful world full of love and hosted by spiritual light beings, and even connecting with long-deceased relatives.

The term for this phenomenon, near-death experience (NDE), was coined by psychologist and author Raymond Moody, M.D., Ph.D. in his best-selling book, *Life After Life* (1975). After interviewing more than 150 people who had gone through a NDE, he observed common elements in the stories told by those who had been revived.

Some of these NDE individuals truly seem enlightened; they end up with an inner sense, an empathetic understanding that was not present before their experience. In other cases, they are left with a kind of oracle/psychic divinity, leaving them with what they call "a sixth sense". Some people claimed to see a "light at the end of a tunnel" at the moment of death. More commonly, people reported being immersed in light, and, in many cases, escorted by a "being" of light to a heavenly and beautiful paradise, where colors were more brilliant than they had ever seen. These beings of light were full of love and compassion, described by some to be angels. In some cases, the person's life was relayed in clear detail, and his or her past actions were reviewed and discriminated upon by themselves, as if from a third-party position.

However, the one consistent and underlying theme of all of these experiences is *light*. It is all about the light; the light is good, the light is love, there are places of light, beings of light, tunnels with light, the light draws them, it is magnetic, and they experience the light as ecstasy, fulfillment, and home.

> **"If you change the way you look at things,**
> **the things you look at change."**
> *Wayne Dyer*

This is nothing new. Many ancient texts include scripture on light's significance. Early Sanskrit writing, for instance, provides information about chakra energy centers within the body that emanate light.

"We are made of light," argues German physicist Fritz-Albert Popp, the leader in scientific research on light emissions, biophotons, emanating from living things. He describes these as ultra-weak chemiluminance signals, stating, "[they] are responsible for simulating 100,000 chemical reactions a second in our cells. Biophotons have a high degree of order, efficiency and coherence, important for highest level of communication clarity."

The significance of light in biology, health, and medicine is just beginning to be understood. Without the light of the sun, of course, we would not exist. But that's only the beginning. In 1986, the late Professor David Bohm, an American theoretical physicist whom Einstein once referred to as his "intellectual successor," described matter as "frozen light," proposing the idea that light can slow down so much that it can become solid.

Through my own interviews and conversations with people who have lived through and written about NDEs, I began to recognize significant patterns that went beyond the elements Moody had found. One of these patterns shows that consciousness travels to a higher, more sensory, and alert dimensional plane that simultaneously occupies the physical one we currently inhabit, as if in a quantitative state.

I call this plane of existence the *Soul Matrix*. This dimensional realm is familiar to figures such as spiritual gurus, shamans, Tibetan monks, transcendental mediators, death experience survivors, and individuals who experience spiritual transformative events. We are part of this plane at this very moment, yet our brains seem to govern us from seeing all those trillions of bits of information that occur around us at any given second, most of which reside outside of our perceived awareness, just so we can function at this planetary level.

When I began reading this information, it was as if I had struck gold. This data seemed to be the most pertinent spiritual information on the planet. I was stunned by the stories people were reporting, and shocked that information of such significance wasn't common, everyday household knowledge.

The more I learned, the more I realized that there were many types of spiritual events sharing the common elements that Moody and I and many others had found, creating threads that, metaphorically, become intertwined into a strong and sturdy rope.

Many of these spiritually transformative events happen to ordinary people, often when they least expect it. For example, we hear stories from people who claim to remember their lives before being born. In some cases, they tell of choosing their birth parents, remembering quantifiable facts and information about them prior to their existence.

14

These are facts that were never told to them, impossible to have been known except by simply occurring to them in a conscious way. Individuals speak of spending time in another place, between lives lived in this physical plane. Still, others speak of interacting with souls, reviewing past lives, and in some cases planning for a new existence, their next incarnation. These reports, which come from many different persons with no exposure to each other, cannot be dismissed as mere coincidence.

Indeed, each of these experiences conveys important spiritual truths that cross all cultures, ideological beliefs, religious affiliations, ethnicities, and class distinctions. They share common elements that make it clear that there is something beyond the life we share here on Earth. These occurrences are known to induce a heightened state of awareness and, in some cases, enhance psychic perception, leaving a everlasting impact on the person. It appears that there is a dimensional connection between these experiences and the very nature of consciousness itself.

"If the infinite had not desired man to be wise,he would not have bestowed upon him the faculty of knowing."
Manly P. Hall

Taking all this into account, I felt compelled to write about metaphysical data from a dispassionate and comparative point of view. This evidence shows our spiritual purpose, the role we are supposed to play here on Earth, determined—and only determined—by ourselves.

Collectively, this evidence sends a clear and powerful message that has the potential to provide humanity with a transcendental perspective of itself. I believe, this understanding can help heighten individual potential, possibly initiating a metamorphosis. Properly understanding it can help humanity transcend from its limiting beliefs in physical capabilities, into higher-dimensional beings with the ability to traverse between this world and loftier planes of love and truth.

Faced with an ever accumulating body of evidence we are challenged to question external dogmas of theocratic belief; and confront the possibility that access to the truth resides within us all. This is the next step in our evolution as a race, if we truly plan to survive as conscious creatures on this planet.

As you will see in the pages ahead, there is growing credible evidence being discovered across the spectrum of scientific inquiry as well as in global spiritual teachings that we are eternal beings. You may come to believe, as I and a growing multitude of others do, that our consciousness continues to perceive and exist even after the physical body dies. I believe we only bring a small part of our soul with us when coming into this physical plane, while the vastly larger other part of us resides in the heavenly realm, the Soul Matrix. We have chosen to forget our connection because it is the only way for us to experience the physical as separate individuals. On the other side, all things are connected and known. Those that cross this threshold of death, and return to tell the story, have begun to see this interwoven spiritual fabric. They are the modern day shamans.

It is now time to move enlightened spiritual truths forward into the new millennium, and evolve into the beings that our spiritual birthright intends.

> **"All matter originates and exists only by virtue of a force... We must assume behind this force the existence of a conscious and intelligent mind. This mind is the matrix of all matter."**
> *Max Planck*

CHAPTER 1
SOUL

"It is within you that the divine lives."
Joseph Campbell

For many of those who have died and come back to life, it's not a lofty experience. In fact, most people do not remember a thing. But for the ones who do, there is a clear and discernible pattern. The pattern establishes a frame of reference from which we can begin to measure this unique experience. That is where this story begins.

The NDE is not exclusive to lofty transcendent experiences. Many individuals who have had spiritual and supernatural experiences believe that during the experience they were part of or connected to another place. Sometimes they describe this place as a dimensional shift of some kind. In *most* cases, they describe going to an extremely loving place.

The question remains: how are NDE and other supernatural and paranormal experiences connected? So many of the elements of these spiritual experiences have commonality, and individuals use similar words to describe the occurrence. Once again, a pattern can be established. At even a larger level, a pattern through all the transcendental, shamanistic, spiritual, paranormal, and supernatural arenas not only describes similar occurrences, but uses many of the same terms to describe the experience that crosses all languages.

The web of these patterns woven together begins to establish a language— possibly the ABC's of a spiritual language. The potential of this new science, or form of communication, to use these terms is enormous, optimistically helping us reach our fullest goodness, allowing us to move onto our highest purpose.

Upon evaluating the data side by side, it becomes clear that these types of experiences have been described in the earliest texts, by ancient philosophers, religions and present new age ideas. They all use words to describe the spiritual event; in proper reference, these words become the foundation for lucid self-understanding. This information points to some intriguing conclusions about both our existence here and our perpetual residence in another dimension. It is truly neither here nor there; we are part of both sides, always.

There are many interesting patterns around each genre of experience, but the one that really stuck with me was how individuals, in their own terms, reported their last memory before jumping into the pool of life. During these memories they remembered the love they came from, but more importantly, trying to do their best to remember that the main point to being alive in the physical is to give love and teach love at every living moment, and not forget that. Some of these reports include individuals speaking of a dense veil between the earthly and heavenly dimension. After passing through it, individuals seem to forget those loving intentions, that were extremely critical - to keep those thoughts and memories intact, that we remind ourself right before we came here.

> **"Weapons cannot destroy it,**
> **Water cannot wet it,**
> **Fire cannot burn it,**
> **Nor can the Wind dry it."**
> *Krishna*

WHAT IS A SOUL?

"The soul is here for its own joy."
Jelaluddin Rumi

Soul is an ancient Greek word traced back to the word *aliolos*, which means iridescent, twinkling, and fast-moving. Many ancient Greek, Sufi, and Gnostic philosophers reported the soul as a moving life force composed of light. In general, the belief was that the physical body is a cage or prison, and it is not until we wake up into who we really are and leave that cage that we understand the true nature of our souls.

Defining the soul beyond the religious and superficial pronouncements typically used is no easy task. After all, how we choose to ultimately define the soul or deny its existence has as much to do with our own particular cultural bias, upbringing, and religiosity as it does with our grasp of language, which, at best, only hints at the magnificent nature of the sublime, given its innate limitations. Language is merely symbolic, and it is often quite useful in the domain of abstract reasoning, whereas the mystery of the soul is beyond the mind to truly conceive. The act of conceiving, after all, is based on thought, not a soul. You could say that we were conceived by a soul before we ever attempted to conceive of a soul.

Members of the Christian church are told that humans were created in the image of God. However, many Christians rarely give more than a passing thought as to what it means to be "created in the image of God". Could we be reading this odd passage too literally, as we tend to do with our religious texts?

We think of images as having form. However, are we really so naïve as to assume God needs to take an anthropomorphic form in line with our own ego's vanity? Or can we look to more spiritual essences as essentially *formless*? Most speculation about matters of the soul remain relatively ignored or only examined by a majority of people, whether secular or non-secular. Regardless of religion, we are left with the most spiritually adroit and wisest among us talking about the soul and matters of the spirit using allegory, parable, and Zen-like *koans*.

Just as our first inhalation of life remains a mystery, so too does the mystery of where the life spirit goes after that last breath is exhaled from our dying lips. Tibetan Buddhist monks spend weeks laying out huge multi-colored sand *mandalas* of extremely intricate geometrical and archetypal patterns only to sweep them quickly away, as soon as they are finally finished. These ascetic monks know all too well that even a long, disciplined life spent meditating and reaching for spiritual wholeness (which the *mandalas* could be said to symbolize) is swept away in the twinkling of an eye, like dust in the wind, when death knocks at one's fleshly door. All of our earthly achievements, cherished memories, accumulated wealth, prestige, and material possessions then appear as illusionary mirages, an ephemeral smoke dissipating in the final breath of life.

This book primarily focuses on this mystery, attempting to explain death through the use of a myriad of peoples' heart-felt stories, as well as interpretations of what they saw, heard, and felt as they approached death, whether consciously or unconsciously. Their testimony gives compelling witness to the absolute certainty and validity of the survival of life after death for them (regardless of their prior beliefs), and it is this mysterious *something* that survives that can rightly be defined as the soul.

Personally, I don't think of the soul as a "thing" at all, in the way that we think of a thing as relatively static and inert. I see the soul more as a kind of quality of energetic and dynamic essence. In metaphysical terms, we could say that the soul is "that eternal, indestructible essence of our true Self or Being, arising from the ineffable, infinite source of all life, light, and love that some call God. So, in the highest sense, the soul partakes in the divine glory of the ultimate fountain of all beings, both manifest and un-manifest.

In the language of poetic analogy (which I feel brings us closest to comprehending the soul), one could say the soul is like a ray from the divine sun, a note from the celestial orchestra of loving creation, or a drop of spiritual water from the ocean of infinite consciousness.

"The soul is light."
Ralph Waldo Emerson

DUALISM

**"We have no evidence whatsoever
that the soul perishes with the body."**
Mahatma Gandhi

For millennia, there has existed the idea that humans have a *dual nature*. That is, humans have both mortal bodies and souls or spiritual aspects, which are usually considered independent of the body. There has been much debate as to whether that soul survives death. The question of the post-mortem survival of consciousness (another term that is often used to name the metaphysical side of this dualism) deserves a serious examination here, through a thoughtful evaluation of the available data.

Now that science has reached the stage of studying subatomic physics in what is called "quantum mechanics," mainstream scientists such as Stephen Hawking, Michio Kaku, and Roger Penrose recognize the high probability that other dimensions or "parallel realities" to our physical universe do exist. The world is now poised for a parallel quantum leap in spiritual evolution that will help us understand ourselves as cosmic co-creators with the divine, almost transforming us from *Homo Sapiens* to *Homo Noeticus,* with the expanded sense of going beyond the physical world. A worldwide shift in consciousness definitely seems to be underway, and, as full participants in this Earthly drama, we need to be ready to help shepherd it into being.

In this book, I bring together spiritual experiences that were significant enough to leave a memorable impact on the individual. When these occurrences happen, they lead people to believe that something profound exists outside of the five senses and the measurable physical world. These experiences, which are generally labeled spiritual or paranormal, are increasingly becoming so widely reported and exhibit so many similarities that many people feel that they serve as proof of the existence of dimensions beyond the physical. Fortunately, and increasingly, intelligent people from the medical and scientific communities are beginning to take a serious look at this.

Some researchers are taking similar information and developing it into a pseudo- or meta-science, outside of the usual mainstream scientific channels. For example, the Near Death Experience Research Foundation, Noetic Science Institute and the Soul Research Institute, exploring the nature of the perception of life as we are familiar with it, as well as how subatomic interactions on a molecular level may actually help support a broader perspective on existence beyond the physical world.

This new science, still in its infancy, is largely fragmented and in need of a coherent and dynamic mythos— or perhaps a reformulation of an ancient mythos. Pierre Tielhard de Chardin's statement nearly 70 years ago, "We are not human beings having a spiritual experience; we are spiritual beings having a human experience," might serve as the rallying cry for this new era.

Unfortunately, the dominance of scientism has *a priori* declaration that concepts related to the "spirit" are invalid. Without a grander sense of the meaning of life and a holistic connection to the eternal presence of the ineffable mystery of *being*, people will inevitably continue to lose their way. Subsequently, spiritual malaise, indifference, and alienation will continue to affect large numbers of the world's population, as it has for centuries.

Paranormal experiences may manifest in a variety of forms. As mentioned, herin I have focused on four of the major categories; 1. NDE 2. LBL (life-between-life regression) 3. Pre-conception memories 4. IACD (induced after-death communication). Yet still including other transformation experiences, (ie:) dreams, unexplained/psychic occurrence because these experiences also weave into the thread of this story.

Using this information, I have outlined interpretative models based on the cause of, and data reported occurring during a transformation spiritual event, which are included as Appendix D, E and F. Appendix F is a graphic interpretative model that represents the birth process into the physical plane, then back to the period between lives, and back into the world as a reincarnated soul.

"All great truths begin as blasphemies."
George Bernard Shaw

SCIENTISM

> "Science without religion is lame.
> Religion without science is blind."
>
> *Albert Einstein*

Ironically, with the rise of *scientism*, the human soul lost some of its hard-won ground as a major component of human nature. For the purposes of this text, let's define "scientism" as "an excessive and exclusive belief in the ability of the scientific method to describe the universe". Beginning in the seventeenth century, when the Copernican, Newtonian, and Cartesian revolutions seized the popular imagination, the Western worldview of secular, scientific materialism denied that consciousness can survive bodily death. In essence, most modern science (established as it was on the primacy of matter) believed that death represented the absolute and final annihilation of the self. Ideas of consciousness existing after death, according to this narrow view, were perceived as mere wishful thinking, self-delusion, or gross superstition.

Thus, scientism left no room for belief in the spiritual, the paranormal, and even the psychological as alternative and equally valid ways to understand our existence. Life was conceived as merely a by-product of random Darwinian evolution and lacked an independent existence apart from matter. In spite of the fact that, for most of human history, the vast majority has continued to believe that human beings have souls that survive in the afterlife, the materialists have nearly drowned out this claim in their insistence that the soul dies with the death of the body.

More recently, the concept of the human soul is making a resurgence in the equation in science. There is now evidence of biomagnetic fields of energy consisting of magnetic properties and biophotons emanating from all living beings that vanishes upon death. In 1920, Duncan MacDougall, an American physician, found a slight loss of weight in the human body at the point of death. Though his work was discredited, to-date no one with current technology has attempted to duplicate his experiment. Since the last half of the twentieth century, there have been scientists exploring the existence of parallel dimensions that occupy the same space as our so-called macro-level space; descriptions of these dimensions involve curious terms like "quanta," "quarks," and "string theory".

The great Chinese Taoist, Chuang Tzu, offers an apt summary of the difficulties faced by any open-minded researcher who would dare risk ridicule, censure, or loss of livelihood by pursuing fringe fields such as the NDE phenomenon. He writes, "You can't discuss the ocean with a well frog— he's limited by the space he lives in. You can't discuss ice with a summer insect— he's bound to a single season. You can't discuss the Way with a cramped scholar— he's shackled by his doctrines."

With the recent rise of scientific inquiry into NDEs and other transcendental spiritual experiences, the case for the hypothesis that human consciousness does indeed survive bodily death has been greatly strengthened.

> **"Great spirits have often encountered...**
> **opposition from weak minds."**
> *Albert Einstein*

THE NDE AS A CATALYST OF HUMAN EVOLUTION

"the NDE is not only an experience of riveting fascination; it is also potentially an extremely *subservice* , threatening to undermine our hard-won secular and scientific worldview."

Kenneth Ring

In the mid-nineteenth century, thanks to the work of people like Alan Kardek, Madame Helena Blavatsky, Frederic Myers, and William Crookes, there was a huge resurgence of interest in the supernatural. During that time, people engaged openly and unabashedly in séances, automatic writing, and work through mediums in an effort to contact the dead. Recent investigations have reported telepathic communication with the deceased through the use of "trance mediums." Skeptical scientists became converts by the sheer weight of the evidence and in light of its then cultural acceptance.

The scientific constructs mentioned above, drawn from the fields of biology, neurology, and biochemistry, have concluded that the death of the physical body is the end of human consciousness, which is said to reside exclusively in the brain. A more moderate approach to these phenomena, from the field of psychology, is quickly gaining ground as a working hypothesis that something does survive thereafter.

One study led by Sam Parnia, assistant professor of medicine at the State University of New York at Stony Brook, explored the memories of over 140 resuscitated individuals who reported their experiences while dead or nearly so, with often very similar results. Parnia additionally explained instances when patients' confirmed consciousness of up to three minutes after their hearts stopped, though the brain shuts down often only twenty to thirty seconds after the heart.

The old nature/nurture conundrum, too, provides strong evidence that the human soul (or something of a nonphysical nature) exists prior to incarnation in the physical form. Child psychologists have never been able to fully explain how children exhibit highly variable personalities, even when they're brought up in the same household. This shows that people are not born as blank slates upon which experience is written, that environmental factors do not account for all (or even most) of human behavior. Rather, people come into the world with an individuality all their own.

The Sufi mystic, Hazrat Inyat Khan, says, "Each soul pre-exists as an electric current, an energy force beyond space and time in a sanctified mental world where love and unity pervade. The soul is entranced into a human body by the love experience of its parents." While we may not fully accept Khan's view of the "mental world," evidence herein points to the conclusion that an energy force pre-dates our entry into this physical plane.

On yet another level, psychology supplies even more important evidence for the existence of other dimensions of reality. The extensive information that has been produced by "trips", by the reaching of altered states of consciousness through the use of drugs, both natural and manufactured, speaks clearly to the transcendental or transpersonal nature of reality. It presumes the existence of other worlds and/or dimensions outside our temporal universe, of which we now have long and storied accounts.

When we move from the "fringe" science of psychological phenomena to the admittedly "beyond the fringe" world of NDE and pre-conception memories, we find there are a number of common threads that begin to weave a bigger picture, a hugely complex picture that is often beyond the ability of the mind to fully comprehend. To even begin to understand the concept of the soul, in fact, we must often ask logic to take a backseat to intuition. Now that quantum physics tells us with certainty that there are indeed other dimensional realities, we can add to the depth of our knowledge, as this book hopes to achieve.

The final answer to the question, "What is the soul?," which is where we began our quest in this chapter, is most likely still beyond our grasp.

"The visible world is the invisible
organization of energy."
Heinz Pagels

CHAPTER 2
PROFOUND JOURNEY

In this chapter, we look more deeply into the entire NDE phenomenon, examining a number of occurrences in depth and look briefly at many others, including a number from celebrities and well-known people of the past and present.

Before we do that, however, it will be helpful to present several of the common elements that seem to be part of almost every NDE that has been reported. These elements include the environment into which near-death experiencers seem to universally find themselves, the beings that inhabit it, and the purpose and meaning that is drawn from these journeys.

When asked, most people would say that, at the very least, death is an unknown process and entity. And, as an unknown, it presents many fearful aspects. Will there be retribution for our sins? Will we have to face our Maker? Or—as many people fear—will there be nothing? Will the consciousness that makes us who we are in this physical existence be extinguished?

Some of these questions are being answered by people who have actually died and come back to life. These people are grouped together and labeled "near-death experiencers" (NDErs), though they vary widely in how and when their experiences occurred. But regardless of how the incidents played out, the reports from near-death experiencers have begun to provide a wealth of information on just what can be expected after we leave this physical plane. The descriptions include such elements as journeying through an energetic passageway (i.e a tunnel) with accompanying sounds of indescribable beauty, "total immersion in a bright light," as experiencing a sense of warmth, peace, and love, a feeling as if one were submerged in the soul's sublime essence. As one NDEr claimed, "It's like I was from there, and I will always be from there, with my existence on earth a brief sojourn."

"Life is a dream walking. Death is going home."
Chinese proverb

"I have yet to meet a single person from our culture...who had powerful transpersonal experiences and continues to subscribe to the materialistic monism of Western science."
Albert Einstein

Raymond Moody's first use of the term "near-death experience" seemed to have opened a floodgate of such reports when his book, *Life After Life*, addressed a concept that entered the minds of millions of people. Moody and other prolific writers in this field allowed people to more readily accept the notion of life after death. Among the patterns he saw among the people he talked with following their NDE was that after their return, they continued to experience marvelous insights and felt their lives to be more deeply meaningful.

P.M.H. Atwater, a researcher of NDEs and herself a veteran of three such incidents, sees our souls' NDE journeys as a life stream. She writes, "It's not water, but it does flow. There is a life stream, and people go in and out. And, when you exit the life stream, that is when you incarnate in a body. When you leave the body, that's when you go back to the life stream."

NDE Environment: is a primary element of the environment of these NDE occurrences, almost always mentioned in the aftermath. The light is always described as brilliant, often with vivid colors in numerous hues, some indescribable. Many people report seeing divine sanctuaries of vivid, rainbow light. Sapphire-blue shimmering waters float in warm cotton-like clouds. They describe marvelous fields of emerald-green grass and perpetually flowering trees that are bathed in this light. All these images tend naturally to blend together into giant mosaics of multi-colored light.

Initial reports of NDEs told of a "house of light", but later reports described larger buildings of light, giant cathedrals built out of blocks that seem to be made of quartz crystal. More recently still, people report seeing entire cities of brilliant golden light shining like lovely gems scattered among the utopian pastoral landscapes. It's almost as though heaven were keeping pace with our growth here on earth! Shades of the wise, old Hermetic axiom comes to mind: "As above, so below," and its addendum, "As within, so without." Although, one in seven cases of people who were clinically dead, spoke of memories of an incomprehensible scary place once they were revived.

Angelic Beings: People often describe being bathed by extremely bright light emanating from the beings that inhabit this celestial place. Some report a spiritual or angelic hierarchy of sorts, wherein these beings emanate more or less light, depending on their rank. The brighter and more vivid the celestial light and the hues seem to indicate differences and strengths of its spiritual vibrations, energy reflecting within, around and out of these beings.

The beings encountered in these experiences invariably emanate love along with the brilliant light. Some people have said that their encounter was with a being who felt like the best friend they've ever had. Many have said that they were met by what they felt was a guardian angel, a friend with an advanced spiritual vibration, who seemed to be there to aid the soul in crossing over to the other side and assist them in their acclimation and adaptation to this strange and wonderful place.

Very often, NDErs will report that, as beings of light, these entities communicate all thoughts telepathically. Thoughts are instantly manifested and travel from the NDEr's light energy to that of the angelic beings, and it seems nothing is lost in translation. Often, one of the first messages communicated in this way was, "Relax, everything is absolutely beautiful." Experiencers are thus put completely at ease, feeling, as is often reported, more at home than they ever had been before in their lives. Many NDErs come to the realization that they have been connected to the source of all knowledge, giving them a sense of omniscience. In fact, there are many descriptions of a great storehouse of knowledge that can be accessed, often referred to as the *Akashic* records, where everything is known about all time periods.

Life Review: The "everything" that is known includes, of course, every detail of every person's life, and one of the common elements that is reported during an NDE is a review of the experiencer's life. This "life review" often happens in the way that we hear about when someone in the physical plane is seconds away from dying: their entire life appears to them, almost as if they were watching a movie.

People suffering from epilepsy claim to experience this life review process often at some point during a seizure. It can be compared with the Charles Dickens' classic, *A Christmas Carol*, in which the curmudgeon, Mr. Ebenezer Scrooge, is forced to view his past misdeeds and their present consequences, all of which radically alters his life for the better, transforming him into a redeeming character. Even though the Dickens tale is fiction, it might have been modeled on reports that existed through the ages and into the nineteenth century of people whose lives "flashed before their eyes" as they came close to death.

As their entire lives pass before them, people will usually experience every emotion that they ever felt in their previous life. In addition, they experience the thoughts and feelings of all those with whom they have interacted, positive and negative. And, in some cases, experiencers report that they relive the physical pain they experienced, as well as the physical pain they inflicted on others. People have reported experiencing the searing pain of bullets searing through another's body of people that had been shot, for instance.

Like Scrooge, experiencers are shown how those actions and the emotions associated with them affected their own lives, as well as the lives of others. Occasionally, similar to what happened to Scrooge, they will even glimpse the way their future lives might have played out. And just as Scrooge became remorseful at the harm he had caused, so the people undergoing this life review begin to feel a degree of remorse for the harm, psychological and physical, that they have caused others. They come to regret how little true love they demonstrated during their lifetime, especially when they realize that the opportunities were there to give it.

As the experiencers watch their life reviews, their interactions with people are also being watched by beings of light. These beings watch entirely without judgment. They will sometimes slow down specific situations and point out details so that the experiencers can observe them more closely. The purpose seems to be only so that the watchers can learn as much as possible about an incident by observing it more objectively, as eyewitnesses rather than participants, and thus see more clearly the "cause and effect" of their actions. In this way, only the NDErs really sit in judgment of themselves.

"You are only asked to look at your life, and to understand…You are not being punished; you are being shown, so that you can learn."
Kenneth Ring

Life reviews can be fairly fast or painfully slow, depending on the life being reviewed. The events are usually presented in chronological order. Some reviews include past lives, though this is rare, and occasionally visions of the future appear—"flash forwards," so to speak. One person described seeing the past in black and white, the future in color.

While these reviews usually focus purely on personal events in the observers' lives, some have reported seeing visions that reveal events with potentially planetary significance. Some of the less desirable events include:

- Increased earthquake or volcanic activity
- Nuclear disasters
- Pole shifts
- Coronal mass ejections
- Worldwide famines due to severe droughts

Some of these glimpses of the future have already come to fruition, while others may occur as an inevitable result of Earth's natural cycles or mankind's ill-conceived actions, maybe hundreds or millions of years in the future. However, there are also reports of visions that predict a new, more spiritually evolved planetary culture emerging out of a period of great cataclysm and chaos.

One common factor that emerges from these NDE encounters with angelic beings in heavenly settings, where the experiencers sit in judgment of their own lives, is that the chief problem among human beings lies in the "negative thought patterns" that seem to besmirch our collective minds. These patterns cause all kinds of havoc in both the physical and psychic environments of our lives. It is as if thought disease becomes contagious in destructive alliances.

Let just one NDE example illustrate this point: one man, newly arrived in this setting, was asked what he had done to benefit or advance the human race. Instantly, he watched as his life flashed before his eyes. To his utter surprise, what he thought that mattered didn't. Everything he held to be important turned out to be totally insignificant. Instead, he saw, the most important thing in life is human relationships. Sharing and giving more love to one another is the most important thing, not material things.

Now let's look at a number of specific NDEs, to discover in detail their patterns, similarities, and uniqueness, and most importantly, the lessons they teach.

> **"When we come to the last moment of this lifetime and we look back across it, the only thing that's going to matter is 'What is the quality of our love?'"**
> *Richard Bach*

HEAVENLY JUDGMENT?

"Humans did not weave the web of life. He is merely a strand of it. Whatever he does to the web he does to himself."

Chief Seattle

Most people who believe that there is life after the body completes its sojourn on earth expect that the soul meets a heavenly board that passes judgment on the life just lived. But for many, that judgment is expected to involve fire and brimstone and other unpleasantries, as has been predicted in various religious philosophies. Those who have been through an NDE report something quite different. There is judgment, to be sure, but there is no judgment from others, we ourselves are our final and only judges. This usually occurs in a group of what is said to be a group of high vibrating luminary beings of light, from moderate to grand in size, depth, knowledge with complete total loving understanding. During that time, it's as if every thought, dimwitted, beautiful act that we ever experienced is before us, as clear as if it were happening in real-time at that second. And it is seen by all...

"Love is the absence of judgment."

Dalai Lama XIV

We are not alone in this process. Rather, everyone is watching, in what has been referred to as a "light board," all the way up to the highest order of beings. Plus, all of our loved ones and associated lifetime connections are also there for us to see in the spiritual realm (what I referred to earlier as the Soul Matrix). All is seen by every soul, and all is known by every soul. It is as if we are completely naked for the world to see—not just our bodies, but our souls. To say "for the world to see" is a huge understatement; it is for the infinite universe to see.

Let us start with Brother Ed Salisbury, a personal friend of mine, whose testimony can be found on YouTube, along with that of many others who have used the You Tube platform to tell of their NDEs. In a nine-minute video he tells of his first NDE, which occurred just after the car he was driving hit a tree. As his body lay shattered, sprawled over the steering wheel of the crumpled car, he testifies that he felt his soul floating into and through the tree, moving through the branches, and coming out above it. He was looking down from what felt like a second story balcony and thought to himself, "That looks like my car." He saw a body slumped over the wheel, smoke billowing everywhere, and people running towards the scene of the accident. His next thought was, "If that is my car, who is that person in it?" Then, when realization hit, he thought, "Oh my God! If that is my body, then WHO I'M I?", perceiving all of this from his vantage point from high above, looking down.

His awareness was then sucked up into a tunnel ("as if a ball of dust into a vacuum hose") and he described feeling the most euphoric sense of ecstasy that he had ever felt, being in a state of "cosmic consciousness." According to Salisbury, a radiant and loving being materialized before his eyes and this being looked like the Jesus that Salisbury had worshiped as an altar boy in his youth. The being was pointing towards a figure sitting up in a chair, appearing to be father God himself. This being radiated so much love that he had trouble breaking eye contact, claimed Salisbury.

Salisbury hesitated at first, and found himself lifted into the lap of this father figure held in an embrace that was "like being immersed in a hot bath after being chilled in the cold." The being that held him gestured towards his feet. Salisbury looked down to see many images strewn at his feet, like photographs from a picture album. In each of the photographs was a memory, in three dimensions, of an incident from his life, each one an incident that had carried with it a feeling of one kind or another, some pleasant, some unpleasant.

> **"What lies behind us and what lies before us**
> **are small matters to what lies within us."**
> *Ralph Waldo Emerson*

In one of the incidents, Salisbury saw himself in his neighbor's garage, stealing empty returnable Coke bottles to get money for the movies. He recalled the smell of the musty garage, felt his heart racing, and heard the glass bottles clanking. He recalled thinking to himself, "Thank God nobody sees me." Yet, now seeing it all over again in God's presence, Salisbury thought, "Oh no, you were there. That's bad." The being's quiet response was, "It's neither good nor bad. It's just a learning of a lesson. Are you through?" He moved to another experience, this time reliving a moment when he had saved a woman from drowning. He could taste the salt water in his mouth from that effort. Asking "wasn't that good"? Once again, he was told, "It's neither good nor bad. In the greater reality, it's just a lesson for learning. Are you through?"

In this way, Salisbury went through every experience that had emotion connection to it, whether the feeling was guilt, shame, pride, vanity, joy, fear, or love. It was all there for him to re-experience and he began to see the larger implications. And after each one, he was asked, "Are you through?"

After all of the experiences had been examined, the question was put before him again. At this point, Salisbury realized he didn't want to go back to the limited physical universe separated from God's infinite love. But, as he made the decision to stay where he was, he reached toward an image and attachment of his mother, thinking, "Let me tell my mom not to worry that I'm okay." That single thought of love for his mother was the catalyst that brought him back to our world.

He awoke instantly in the hospital, where he had been in a coma for two weeks. His mother was at the foot of his bed. He began to describe his experiences to her and the others who attended to him. The doctors tried to convince him that he had hallucinated the entire thing. However, deep in his gut he knew better. He could remember how he had felt when reliving his experiences, the fear and shame. But more significantly, he could also *feel* the emotional and mental processes of others with whom he had interacted, and the pain that he had caused others by his behavior. Those feelings had never been part of his understanding before. They had come to him as a result of the "lessons for the learning" that he had been shown.

Salisbury's story of his first NDE, which has been videotaped and posted to YouTube, remains at this point the most popular NDE on the site, nearing a million hits. It beautifully illustrates the Life Review and demonstrates how learning such otherworldly lessons can make a difference in a person's life. In addition to his, there are literally thousands of similar enlightening stories one can find in books, articles, and on the internet.

> **"All that we are is the result of what we have thought.
> The mind is everything. What we think, we become."**
> *Maharishi Mahesh Yogi*

ULTIMATE DEAD GUY

"The quickest way to change the world is to be of service to others… Each of us doing that and working together we change the world one inner person at a time."
Dannion Brinkley

On September 17, 1975, at 7:05 p.m., 25 year-old Dannion Brinkley's life changed forever. A bolt of lightning struck his head and ran down the length of his spine, throwing him violently into the air and stopping his heart. He dipped in and out of death, despite doctors' use of electric paddles and adrenaline shots to his heart. Brinkley later recounted: "You burn and hurt like hell, as if you drank battery acid. You're on fire. You don't know what to do, where to go, or what to think about it. Then, all of a sudden, you lift out of your body, and you're in this blue-gray, soft, loving, comfortable place feeling a sense of calm familiarity like you've never felt before. You begin to think how you were so dumb to fall from grace to begin with as to be born into a physical life."

This experience and a second NDE are described in Brinkley's 1994 book, *Saved by the Light*. He has since had a third NDE and has authored two more books about his experiences. Here is how Brinkley himself describes how his worldview changed after his NDE. Before he was struck by lightning, he says, "I thought that this kind of thing was hogwash. I thought it was not only hogwash; it was stupid because I couldn't comprehend it. Well, one day I never believed a single word of it, and the next day I was dead and experienced everything I never believed."

"A mind stretched by a new idea can never go back to its original dimensions."
Oliver Wendell Holmes

Most of us would agree with Brinkley's assessment that we come into this physical reality and have virtually no knowledge of our eternal soul. But, because of his experience, he adds, "We are not sent here to suffer. We only choose to suffer because we grow bitter under adverse conditions. However, we're meant to overcome our adversity. We bring into our lives what we most need to grow and expand our spiritual nature, creating conflict as a test to see if our love can endure. Our so-called problems arise so that we can learn how to love more, be more compassionate." He feels that we are all connected, and we exist in an ever-unfolding universe filled with wonderment and beauty. He adds, "We are not small and insignificant. We are very important, purposeful, powerful, and loving beings at heart."

For Brinkley, one of the most interesting aspects of an NDE occurred when he was first conscious of lifting up and out of his body. As he put it, "What we are taught [about death] is great fear. Well, not only is it interesting that you have consciousness [upon dying], you are amazed at how much smarter, brighter, and keener your senses become. What a sense of humor you develop when you realize that you're dead, being still alive. You realize that death, as we know it, is a joke, it's something to laugh at."

Another feature of Brinkley's experiences that he reported was the ability to see through people: "I began to truly understand when they say an atom is about 98% empty space because physical bodies were transparent. You could see some identity, but what you really saw was a series of points, emanating glorious color and movement. Energy would blend together, and there would be one big bouquet of beautiful floral hues of intense color."

Perhaps one of the most interesting comments from Brinkley came after his third NDE, when he reported, "I was in the blue-gray place longer than I ever was in the first two NDEs. So, I had a chance to look to my left and look to my right, and I could see waves of consciousness, energy, and spiritual beings. There were literally dozens of different levels. There were some levels that you could say were populated with extraterrestrials in that they didn't look like other people."

When we look at the many recent developments in physics, metaphysics, and quantum mechanics, especially in light of what we hear from those who have come back from death, as Brinkley has, we start to see where science and spirituality begin to merge. It suddenly becomes clear that the physical world is the biggest illusion of all. Brinkley says: "It is a joke to think that anything is truly solid, as we believe it to be. We construct much of our existential reality in our minds. What the NDE teaches us is that physical existence, as we perceive it, is a very minor part of the overall picture. What I've learned to realize, through three of these NDEs, is how awesome we really are. We are beings of radiant light, magnificent, beautiful creatures, who are only encapsulated in this physical body. We are not physical; it's a part of us, but it's not who *we* are."

Based on his multiple NDEs, Brinkley refers to himself as "the Ultimate Dead Guy." His experiences have made huge and beneficial changes in his life, although he does not recommend that others try to replicate these NDEs, stating, "It destroyed my entire world as I knew it." However, these experiences have shown him that we are great, powerful, spiritual beings of light, living in a seemingly physical world with a certain degree of dignity, grace, and purpose.

Brinkley further purports that each one of us, as a soul, chose to be born. He says, "We choose to come to this world, in order to make changes for the betterment of humanity (see Appendix A), knowing that we are capable of making a real difference. Each of us has created our lives with as many obstacles and challenges as we needed along the way and the options and possibilities for overcoming these challenges. So, when you look at how screwed up your life is, just remember that you chose to come here."

We, too, chose to be alive in this time, in this place, and in this body. We have been given an abundance of gifts and talents, and a glorious opportunity to use these gifts and talents, each in our own way and using our individual power. Our quest must be to discover how to live our lives as artfully as possible, and one vital aspect of living *artfully* is to discover and develop these talents to produce the greatest possible good for the greatest number of people.

> **"There are no mistakes, no coincidences.**
> **All events are blessings given to us to learn from."**
> *Elizabeth Kubler-Ross*

HEAVENLY BOY

"My Kingdom is not an earthly kingdom."
John 18:36

As one might expect, the near-death phenomenon is experienced not only cross-culturally, but also across all age groups. The NDEs of children have just as profound effects on them as their adult counterparts, but there are invariable differences in the pattern of the experience for children, since children process things quite differently than adults do.

One such youngster, four year-old Colton Burpo, whose journey to heaven and back has recently gained a lot of attention, illustrates this perfectly. His story is told in the book, *Heaven Is for Real*, published in 2010, and, four years later, in a movie based on the book. Though Colton never flat-lined or died, he underwent a forty-five-minute surgery during which he was very close to death. Shortly after he recovered from surgery, he began to speak about his experience. What he had to say to his father, Todd Burpo, pastor of a small local church, and to members of his family and his father's congregation, has affected them—and now the millions who have been exposed to the story—in astounding ways.

Young Colton had been sick for several days, but his illness had been dismissed as merely another instance of a flu bug that had been going around at the time. Finally, after five days, when it became clear that his symptoms were not abating, a re-examination indicated that he was in an advanced stage of appendicitis. He was rushed into surgery, but, because of the delay, it soon became clear that his chances of survival were bleak.

Thankfully, Colton's story has a happy outcome. After surgery, within a day of being on the edge of death, he returned to his usual chipper self. The medical staff at the hospital, those who had been unwilling to give the family false hope about Colton's chances during the operation, came to his bedside afterward to witness what they termed a "miracle": this small boy who had been so near-death had recovered so completely.

But his miraculous revival was only one small part of his story. Soon after recovering from his near-fatal illness, Colton began talking about the experience, and the things he had to say were nothing short of astounding. One of the first things he reported was that angels had sung to him. Moreover, he told his parents, he had met his great-grandfather and a miscarried sibling whom he had previously known nothing about. Not only that, he said he had also met with Jesus and had talked to him.

As noted, Colton did not actually die on the operating table, as the case in some NDEs, even though he came close to death before and during his surgery. But clearly his soul was busy during those minutes when he was not conscious. As he revealed more and more about what he had experienced, those who heard his words could only react in astonishment and—initially, at least—in disbelief. All the talk they were hearing about Colton being out of his body, about angels, about talking with Jesus, about the beautiful place he was in, Heaven—coming from a four-year-old, must had only consisted of a child's dream.

But Colton kept talking. During surgery, he said, he looked down at the doctor and saw everything that occurred in the operating room. He could see his mother praying and talking on the phone, encouraging others from their church to pray as well. He could see his father in a small room near the operating room, and it was clear to Colton that his father was very angry. He saw him raging at God, asking why God would take his son after all his service to the Lord. In fact, Colton said, while he was in Heaven, he prayed for his dad.

After he told this to his parents, both of them confirmed that what Colton saw was exactly what occurred during the time of the surgery. They were dumfounded. Now they had to reconsider everything else Colton had said. Was all of that real as well? Once Colton began conveying facts that were undeniable, but that he clearly could not have known, it became nearly impossible to dismiss his claims.

Ultimately, what Colton relayed raised a number of crucial questions. There was the question of prayer. During the ordeal, Todd, a pastor with strongly held beliefs, along with his wife and the church parishioners, had offered numerous and constant prayers for Colton.

Had these prayers been a factor in the child's recovery? One of the things Colton said was that, during the operation, Jesus had worked through the doctor to save him.

Colton also had much to say about Heaven, which for him was a very real place. There, he said, everyone looked like angels, all of them with a light above their head and wearing robes in the most magnificent colors. He pointed out that all of the beings wore different colors, but Jesus was the only one wearing purple.

Details like these are similar to those reported by other people who have had near-death or spiritual experiences. As more and more people return from journeys "back home," they add to our understanding of experiences in the non-physical realm. Can we continue to be content to treat Heaven as a metaphor when these experiences all seem so similar, and so real?

When Colton talked about meeting his great-grandfather in Heaven, he commented that, "he's really nice," referring to him in the present tense. Todd presented his son with many questions about this man. For example, he asked if, when it got dark, Colton had gone home with Grandpa. The boy's response was, "It doesn't get dark in Heaven. It's always bright."

Todd showed Colton several pictures of his grandfather as an older man, but Colton repeatedly said that they did not show the man he had met. At one point upon looking at the pictures, he said, "No one wears glasses in heaven." On a sudden whim, Todd asked his mother to send a picture of his grandfather when he was younger. When Colton saw it, he immediately recognized it as the great-grandfather with whom he had chatted in heaven. He went on to say, matter-of-factly, "Nobody is old in heaven."

And at another time when he was talking about his grandpa, he said, "If you don't go to heaven, you don't get a new body." This statement sounds as if he is referring to reincarnation, a concept in which the ancient gnostic Christians believed. Again, we must question our own reluctance to accept reincarnation as part of the normal cycle of our existence.

Because of Todd's involvement with the Church and Colton's attendance at Sunday school, the boy had been exposed to the basic spiritual concepts and scripture. But after his near-fatal bout of appendicitis, Colton's understanding of these ideas became quite lucid and detailed. These basic religious ideals seem to have provided him with a language that enabled him to explain his journey using this familiar religious context.

> **"There are innumerable definitions of God...**
> **because manifestations are innumerable."**
> *Mahatma Gandhi*

Oftentimes, people who have had similar experiences cannot explain the concepts, or find the words to explain what has happened to them. Thus, we see that spirituality through a shared religious platform helps us understand our deeper connection to our source, however we choose to name it.

As a result of information taken from Colton's experience and from the many other similar spiritual experiences happening to children and adults alike around the world, we are learning that we don't necessarily need a religious context to understand our connection to the infinite love source— our home, soul, true self, and the place of love where we are all connected for eternity.

This experience changed Colton, the Burpo family, and the members of the church where Todd is a pastor. Before Colton's experience, Todd believed in what he was telling his parishioners, but he readily admitted that he felt some of the concepts he spoke about were metaphorical. After what occurred to his son, however, he is now certain that Heaven is a real place. What his son saw brought new light to his understanding of our connection to eternity.

With the success of the book, *Heaven Is For Real*, and the release of the motion picture, this little boy's experience has reached millions. With or without its underlying religious context, the truth of what has been revealed is evident, and the world seems to be ready to receive this truth. The veil between heaven and earth is becoming thinner.

We are a race of beings who seek to understand these fundamental truths of the infinite love source from which we come, and of our own connection to it. More importantly, as a race, we need these truths to take the next step in our inevitable social evolution on Earth.

"Mind and intelligence are woven into the fabric of our universe in a way that altogether surpasses our understanding."

Freeman Dyson

CHILDREN OF THE NDE

> *"The only real death that ever occurs*
> *is when a dream we cherish dies."*
> *P.M.H. Atwater*

P.M.H. Atwater is one of the best researchers in the growing field of the NDE phenomenon. Having experienced a few NDEs herself, her pioneering efforts have produced what I consider to be the definitive book on this fascinating subset of the NDE, *Children of the New Millennium*.

During the course of her decades-long research, Atwater has spoken to approximately 3,000 adult NDErs, and nearly 300 young NDErs, mostly between the ages of 3 to 15 years old. She has also conducted follow-up interviews when the children reached adulthood, and has succeeded in putting their NDE into a greater contextual perspective.

In analyzing NDEs, whether of children or adults, Atwater finds an NDE incident can be placed in one of four categories: the initial experience, the unpleasant experience, the heavenly experience, and the transcendent experience. Let's take a close look at each of these categories, and also at the frequency with which each is experienced by adults and children.

The Initial Experience: This type of NDE, which Atwater occasionally called the "non-experience," is characterized by a kind of "dark loving nothingness." It usually involves no more than a brief out-of-body journey, with few sensory images experienced by the subject, though voices are sometimes reported. This type of NDE is reported by 76% of children NDErs, compared to 20% of adult NDErs.

The Unpleasant Experience: This type of NDE, also called "hellish," the subject encounters a kind of nightmarish haunting or indifferent void-like purgatory. Atwater's analysis shows that these seem to occur only in cases where an individual harbors deeply-repressed feelings of guilt, fear, anger, and self-loathing— in other words, the feelings that would cause someone to attempt suicide. These scary occurrences only account for only 3% of children NDErs and 15% of adult NDErs.

The Heavenly Experience: This type is the largely familiar "heavenly" or pleasant experience, where subjects have loving reunions with deceased family members, spiritual guides, angels, and religious figures. Colton Burpo's experience is a prime example of this type of NDE. Experiences of this type often seem to provide personal reassurance and validation to those who report them. In Atwater's research, they occur in 19% of children NDErs, compared to 47% of adult NDErs.

The Transcendent Experience: The last type of NDE takes the whole experience to a much higher and more complex level. Transcendent NDEs are characterized by what Atwater terms "other-worldly dimensions," "revelations," and "universal truths." Both Dannion Brinkley and Reverend Salisbury seem to have experienced this type of NDE. Only 2% of children report experiences of a transcendent nature, compared with 18% of adults.

In the most basic of observable changes, regardless of which type of NDEs reported, Atwater states that, following their NDE, adult experiencers tended to become "more child-like," whereas very young experiencers generally became "more adult-like." Both usually returned with the idea that they had a mission to fulfill, but adults seemed to act with a greater sense of urgency, whereas most children tended to be more methodical and much slower to act upon any perceived mission.

Atwater found that children NDErs seemed to undergo a more radical transformation in consciousness than did the majority of adults. Her hypothesis is that this difference is probably due to the fact that children's brains are still developing. She describes this transformation as a kind of "second birth," and likens it to a spirit/brain shift.

This shift takes place in the limbic portion of the brain, which is the "emotional" or "feeling" center, responsible for regulating the body's immune system and filtering memories into short and long-term recall. In terms of NDE neurophysiology, the limbic system has long thought to be the gateway to expanded levels of consciousness, psychic functions, and heart-based (i.e. intuitive) awareness.

Since the first half of the twentieth century, there has been a global jump in the I.Q. of children, amounting to around 30 points (as reported in the March 2013 edition of *Monitor,* the journal of the American Psychological Association). Atwater was startled to find that, in the case of children NDErs, this jump is especially pronounced, noting that roughly half of those children who have experienced the near-death phenomenon fall within this same score range, upward to 150 and higher. This jump in I.Q. is almost always sudden and corresponds to the timing of their NDE.

There's no doubt that post-NDE neurophysiological changes are significant, and it's not surprising that they are particularly marked among children. In addition to the heightened intelligence already mentioned, there are a number of other specific characteristics attributed to children NDErs, including:

- Sensitivity to light and sound
- Increase of allergies
- Strong spiritual inclinations
- Connection with nature and animals
- Psychic enhancements
- Increased creativity

In many respects, the NDE is tougher for children to cope with than adults. After all, children often do not possess a framework of reference through which to understand their experiences, or the life experience to have the wherewithal to navigate the complexities and profundities that they've encountered.

In addition, their changes in behavior, stimuli sensitivities, psychic abilities, and spiritually oriented interests often cause their peer groups to label them as "weird," and they are often ridiculed and abused even by their own family members for being different. According to Atwater, "one-third of the child experiencers ... admitted to having problems with alcohol within five to ten years after their episode. Almost to a person, they claimed that undeveloped social and communication skills were the culprit, along with the inability to understand what motivated family members and friends." Some 41% desired to return to the other side, and 21% even attempted suicide in an effort to get back.

Coming to terms with their brief brushes with the divine only to be forced to return to the alienated miseries of our indifferent world clearly isn't exactly easy, especially for children. One of these children, Beverly A. Brodsky, who had an NDE during a tonsillectomy when she was around 8 years old, said afterwards, "I had no childhood after my near-death experience. I felt cheated." Clara Lane, who had an NDE at age ten during a bout with appendicitis, echoed this sentiment: "I never felt free to talk about this when I was younger. People didn't and still don't believe things like this." However, Clara seems to have been able to cope with her experience at least to some extent, for she ends her statement by saying, "But I know the truth, and that's what's important."

The good news is that, if these children can survive the societal alienation, peer ridicule, and feelings of isolation within their own families, as Clara seems to have done, they often reach adulthood with a greater sense of purpose, spiritual integrity, and love of life's bounty. Atwater has found that nearly half of NDErs end up realizing exactly what their mission is on Earth, and end up achieving it. More than half have "no regrets" about their NDE.

I have hope that we will begin to be more open to young NDErs, since social acceptability, empathy, and encouragement are what these kids need the most in their lives after NDE. Michael Kelley, who had an NDE at two years of age after falling out of a moving car, sums up quite succinctly the truth behind his experience:

"We live to execute a properly conceived life plan whereby each human being becomes an artistic genius. The *light's* knowledge and love are the paint and the inspiration that we, God's little brushes, apply to Earth's giant canvas, allowing each of us to add our few unique brush strokes to God's Grand Painting of Life."

> **"Man's status in the natural world is determined, therefore, by the quality of his thinking."**
> *Manly P. Hall*

> "The body is only a garment...When you give up this
> bodily dress at death you do not change.
> You are just the same, an immortal soul."
> *Paramahansa Yogananda*

Many adults who experience NDEs do not want to discuss what happened to them. This is largely in part because they are aware, as children often aren't, that there is a large population who will label them as "different". When an NDEr is a celebrity, this fear can often be large enough to ensure that the experience is never revealed. However, some celebrities perceive their fame as providing a platform with which they can perhaps use to help change public perception of NDEs.

One of these celebrities, Hollywood actress Sharon Stone, became an ardent humanitarian activist following her own NDE, subsequently supporting several philanthropic organizations to help people all over the world. Stone nearly died after suffering from acute internal bleeding caused by the bursting of an artery at the base of her skull. She said the rupture hit her so hard that she felt like she'd been shot, and, in the aftermath, she says, "I had a real journey that took me to places both here and beyond and affected me so profoundly that my life will never be the same." As a result of her experience, Stone says that she is now not afraid of dying. She believes that death is a gift and a very beautiful thing.

Stone's story is only one of many appearing in the blog, "Near-Death Experiences of the Rich and Famous," created by Kevin Williams in 2014, webmaster of the website near-death.com.

Among the others he mentions in the blog is 36 year-old actress Jane Seymour, who received an injection of penicillin to combat a severe case of influenza. The drug brought on a severe allergic reaction, which led to her NDE. Seymour recalls seeing herself lying on a bed while people tried to resuscitate her. When she saw her life flash before her eyes, her first thought was, "I don't want to leave my children." She began to plead with God: if He would let her return, she would never again take his name in vain. She also remembers pleading with the doctors to bring her back. Ultimately, she found herself back in her body.

Williams discusses at some length the near-death experience of Peter Sellers and its effects on the actor. On the set of his last movie, *Being There*, Sellers admitted privately to his colleague Shirley MacLaine that he had had an NDE fifteen years earlier, in 1964, when he suffered a series of eight heart attacks. He was actually surprised to discover that MacLaine didn't think he was nuts.

> **The soul is everlasting, and its learning experience is lifetime after lifetime.**
> *Shirley MacLaine*

Sellers told her that, when he was out of his body, he saw a bright loving light above him that had a powerful attraction for him and that he thought must be God. Seller's family and friends found him to be more spiritually-oriented after that event, and Sellers himself called it the single most important experience of his life. However, even though he felt that he had lived many lifetimes before, he never fully understood his purpose in this lifetime. Sellers died in 1980.

Another person who found it difficult to talk about NDE was the late actress Elizabeth Taylor. According to Jean Ritchie's 1996 book, *Death's Door*, Taylor spoke openly while appearing on *Larry King Live* of undergoing surgery in the late 1950s and being pronounced dead for a period of five minutes. During her experience, Taylor reported being connected with her late husband, Mike Todd, who had died very recently. She says that it was Todd who told her that she could not stay with him at that time, and that she still had work still to do and needed to return. When she came back, there were eleven people in the room, and her death certificate had already been filled out!

William Petersen, actor on the television series *CSI: Crime Scene Investigation*, nearly died when he cut off one of his fingers during a performance in a Chicago theater. In Lisa Wade McCormick's 2009 book, *Near-Death Experiences: The Unsolved Mystery*, Petersen claims that while in the emergency room, having lost a lot of blood, he found himself on what he called "the 'All That Jazz' escalator, with a long tunnel and a lot of white light". He remembers what he calls "a dominant male voice" telling him that it was not his time, and that he needed to get off the escalator because he still had things to do. His reaction is fascinating: "Something in me changed, a sort of knowledge that somewhere on the other side, it's good."

But he also had to deal with the skepticism of those he told about the experience: "For weeks, the more I talked about it, the more freaked out people got. Some of them were like, 'Okay, whatever: You took too many drugs.'"

On his blog, Williams briefly discusses a number of other film and music industry personalities who experienced NDEs and elected to talk about it. It's interesting to note that three of those he names had their experiences as children: actor James Cromwell, perhaps best known for his role as the farmer in the movie *Babe*, nearly drowned at age five and describes his entire life following the incident as a "mystical event."

Actor Louis Gossett, Jr., has had several NDEs, including one at age twelve. He was playing baseball, fell into a deep hole, and found himself in a tunnel filled with bright light. Finally, Rebecca DeMornay, nearly died from a peptic ulcer when she was with her mother in Mexico at the age of seven. She remembers waking up and going to the window where she saw barefoot children dancing around an old-fashioned lamppost while snow fell around them. Later, she realized that what she had seen could have not actually happened and now feels that what she saw was not real at all.

More stories from Williams' blog provide details that corroborate the similarities of these NDEs. Actor Donald Sutherland was suffering from a massive fever, when he recalled how, "suddenly all of that distress seemed to evaporate." He found himself floating above his body surrounded by a soft light and gliding through a long tunnel, before returning to his body. Later, his doctors told him that he had died for a period of time.

While filming an episode of "CHiPs," TV actor Eric Estrada was in a serious motorcycle accident. He recalls being in a long corridor of bright light, hearing beautiful music, and feeling a sense of great peace. But something seemed to be blocking his progress on this path, and finally a voice told him that he had to go back. Though he had achieved a great deal, he was told, he had not yet found personal happiness and peace of mind, and so he needed to return. Add to these accounts those of such luminaries as Larry Hagman, Gary Busey, Robert Pastorelli, Tony Bennett, Burt Reynolds, Chevy Chase, Eric Roberts (who coincidentally played Dannion Brinkley in the TV movie), Ozzy Osborne, George Lucas (in coma – near fatal auto accident), and there is clearly a significant proportion of celebrities who have experienced NDEs and decidedly chosen to talk about them. This makes one think: How many celebrities and public figures experienced NDE's and did *not* choose to talk of them?

There is no doubt that public perception can affect a celebrity's impact at the box office and entire livelihood and legacy. That is one of the risks inherent in the line of work they have chosen. It is natural *not* to want to give the media any more personal information about themselves than they are required to for their careers. Therefore, their concerns and apprehension over speaking about such unusual occurrences are understandable.

"Continue to grow and evolve."
Mahatma Gandhi

HISTORICAL NDEs

**"There is a change and migration of the soul
from this world to another."**

Plato

Though little can be known of NDEs historically beyond what exists in the literature, there have been numerous instances of historical personages undergoing events that could be categorized as NDEs and that profoundly affected them.

Benjamin Franklin is a prime example. In 1727, at the age of 21, he fell severely ill with pleurisy and nearly died. He writes of this experience in his autobiography: "My distemper was a Pleurisy, which very nearly carried me off; I suffered a good deal, gave up the point in my own mind, and was rather disappointed when I found myself recovering; regretting in some degree that I must now some time or other have all that disagreeable work to do over again."

"A man is not completely born until he is dead."

Benjamin Franklin

This account in his own words does not actually describe what he experienced during his illness, but he seems to exhibit some of the characteristics that we have seen in other NDErs, notably his disappointment in recovering from his sickness.

It was just a few months after this harrowing event that he went on to create the Junto, a group of like-minded aspiring artisans and tradesmen who sought to improve themselves while improving their communities. In his words, the Junto was "the best school of philosophy, morals and politics that then existed in the province," also known as the American Philosophy Association. The friendships formed through this organization, as well as the ideas it spawned, led Franklin to lead an active political and scientific life through which he became one of the founding fathers of America and a key figure in physics for his discoveries in electricity. Though the connection is not explicit, one wonders whether without the NDE to jump-start his creative life, he would have ever achieved all he ultimately accomplished.

Abraham Lincoln suffered two major accidents, both of which could qualify him as a survivor of a NDE. Before he turned seven, he nearly drowned when he fell into a river and was grabbed by a friend. His friend pounded on his chest as water poured out of his mouth, and he finally regained consciousness. The second incident occurred when Lincoln was kicked in the head by a horse. In an 1860 biographical sketch he wrote about himself, Lincoln described the event as follows: "In my tenth year I was kicked by a horse, and apparently [sic] killed for a time." Shortly after his NDE, he had an insatiable craving for knowledge and devoured every book he laid his hands on. In many cases of NDE, it is common for people to have a heightened desire for reading and learning. Lincoln, of course, became the 16th president of the United States and signed the Emancipation Proclamation which ultimately led to the abolishment of slavery in the United States.

> **"The day science begins to study non-physical phenomena,**
> **it will make more progress in one decade**
> **than in all the previous centuries of its existence."**
> *Nikola Tesla*

Someone who made it clear that his NDE was responsible for his many accomplishments was the renowned inventor, Nikola Tesla. Born in 1856, he was a sickly child prone to hallucinations and vivid dreams, which must have been exacerbated by the death of his older brother when Tesla was five. At the age of 18, he contracted cholera and nearly died several times. What he might have seen during these NDEs, if in fact, he saw anything at all, is not known, but Tesla said years later that the period of illness is when he "truly became an inventor." He reported an intense expansion of his physical senses, to the point where he couldn't even stand to be touched. After his recovery, he was able to envision the ideas that would make him arguably the 20th century's greatest inventor. Tesla was instrumental in the development of the radio, the induction motor, wireless technology, and alternating current (AC), which is used in electrical grids around the world, among many other amazing inventions.

Incidentally, Thomas Edison, who was a contemporary and well-known rival of Tesla's, never reported having what could be called an NDE. However, according to various sources, including the book

Edison: Inventing the Century by Neil Baldwin, as he approached the hour of his actual death he reportedly emerged from a coma, opened his eyes, looked upwards, and said "It is very beautiful over there."

On February 10, 1908, when he was nearly 40 and beginning to become a highly visible figure in the nonviolent fight for civil rights in both India and South Africa, Mahatma Gandhi was severely beaten by a group protesting against his political activities. When he regained consciousness, Gandhi reported an intense recognition of the separateness of the soul from the body. He realized, he said, that suffering came only to those who were too closely attached to their bodies and unaware of the eternal and nonphysical nature of their soul.

Once an individual becomes completely free of fear, convinced of the soul's immortality, that individual becomes virtually fearless and unstoppable. With his vision of the infinite, Gandhi went on to become the key figure in India's liberation from British colonial rule, while proving nonviolent revolution is possible. Without such a powerful NDE vision and this enlightened understanding of the soul's true condition, it is quite possible that Gandhi's peaceful and successful revolution against British Empire might not have happened.

> **"Nothing in life is to be feared, only understood."**
> *Madame Marie Curie*

Albert Einstein Ph.D. was utterly obsessed with light. He was convinced that light was the one quality that connected all things in existence. He wrote the Special Theory of Relativity ($E = mc^2$). Einstein's theory sought to prove a deep connectivity with all things in the universe that is fundamental to the nature of light. It describes how matter and light are interchangeable aspects of the same basic substance, existing at different vibratory frequencies. It is said that Einstein fell terribly ill and nearly died, the date of this incidence is not clear.

> **"The most beautiful thing we can experience is the mysterious. It is the source of all true art and science."**
> *Albert Einstein*

Carl Jung, Ph.D., the brilliant depth-psychologist, experienced a NDE in 1944 when he suffered a heart attack. His profound brush with death left a deep impression on him. Describing his NDE in *Memories, Dreams, Reflections*, he wrote:

"This experience gave me a feeling of extreme poverty, but at the same time of great fullness. There was no longer anything I wanted or desired. I existed in objective form; I was what I had been and lived. At first the sense of annihilation predominated, of having been stripped or pillaged, but suddenly that became of no consequence. Everything seemed to be past; what remained was a *fait accompli* without reference back to what had been. There was no longer any regret that something had dropped away or been taken away. On the contrary: I had everything that I was, and that was everything."

Later, in a letter to a friend, Jung wrote, "Death is the hardest thing from the outside, as long as we are outside of it. But, once you get a taste of such completeness, peace, and fulfillment, you don't want to return." He felt that there were great possibilities for overcoming our normal limitations to fully develop such things as telepathy and precognition. Some of his most profound writings came in the immediate years following his heart attack.

Jung was arguably the most important researcher into the deeper levels of the subconscious mind and of the symbolism of dreams. Moreover, his work became the foundation for an understanding of the collective unconscious mind that influences how we think about our daily reality.

"The unconscious psyche believes in life after death."
Carl Jung

Joseph Murphy was a prolific writer, author of over two dozen books on subjects ranging from the subconscious, religion, and ESP. At the age of 28, he suffered an illness that rendered him unconscious for several days. During this time, he reported that he was out of his body and able to pass through closed doors, that he had connected with deceased relatives, and could go anywhere in the world just by thinking about it. "There were no boundaries," he wrote. "Everything seemed to be alive, and I had no sense of time. I felt free, exalted, and rapturously ecstatic." He was furious about returning from this beautiful transcendent state. He believed that at death we move into a higher dimensional state and that death is actually a birth-day into this transcendent realm. After his experience, he was completely confident that we are infinite beings.

**"Death is nothing more than a doorway,
something you walk through."**
George Ritchie

From these reports on NDEs and their consequences, these exceptional human beings make it clear that having a near-death experience leads to a much deeper understanding of the fundamental underpinnings of the universe.

In summary, the historical persons that we have looked at in this section may have used unconsciously the spiritual knowledge that came from their NDEs to make tremendous impacts on the progress of humanity's evolution and knowledge. Perhaps this is a small sample of what happened throughout history, possibly acting as a catalyst for mankind's consciousness evolution. With this wisdom available to us, doesn't it seem foolish not to learn as much as we can about our multi-dimensional spiritual identities so that we can better appreciate and explore these wonderful inner realms of which we are all inherently a part?

"No one knows whether death may not even turn out to be one of the greatest blessings of human beings. And yet people fear it."
Socrates

DIMENSIONAL ASPECTS

"Do you remember how electrical currents and 'unseen waves' were laughed at? The knowledge about man is still in its infancy."
Albert Einstein

For over thirty years, Dr. Robert Brumblay has been saving lives. He is an emergency room physician and has successfully revived many dying patients on the operating table in the ER. Over the years, he has worked with a large number of patients who were clinically dead for a time, who then came back and told amazing stories of their NDEs. Brumblay's curiosity finally got the better of him, when his own wife had a NDE. He has now become dedicated to trying to understand the phenomena that occur during the NDE and the similarities with Out of Body Experiences (OBEs) and extrasensory perception (ESP).

One of Brumblay's interests is trying to understand the visual phenomena or perspective that occurs during the near-death experience. Near-death experiencer's will come back saying that they were looking at the room from near the ceiling. But what is amazing is that they state that they were able to see the near and far side of objects. If they were looking at a table they are able to see the top and bottom at the same time. This unusual perspective doesn't stop there, people in this state also claim that walls become very translucent and are able to be seen through easily.

A patient of Brumblay revived said that during his NDE he experienced intensely beautiful colors. It appeared to him as if all the light was coming to him through a prism, and he was at the center of it. Soon, he became aware that he was looking at colors beyond the visible light spectrum, and he felt his sight stretch out omni-directionally in a kind of 360-degree vision, also know as veridical perception. There was also a feeling of being filled with divine love and a desire to remain in that state forever.

Brumblay pointed out one thing that they notice is that there is no gravity in the region of where they are drifting during their near-death experience. At some point physicists may find that gravity is not a strong force out in that region. But on the other hand electromagnetic fields have been reported to trouble people during a near-death experience. So it seems as if there is some extension of electromagnetic phenomena that goes beyond our three dimensional space into hyper dimensional space. These two variables could very well be constants needed for modern physicists to begin to analyze this new science. Brumblay is humble about his brilliant and pioneering observations. Here is a man who has taken phenomena full of many small dots of information and started to draw the lines in-between.

Brumblay feels that if the area of religion and spirituality converged with the area of science we may very well come up with explanations for these phenomena that do violate the laws of nature but are perfectly in tune with science we have yet to discover. There are a number of unresolved scientific mysteries in physics when adding alternative dimensionality to the equations. Brumblay's goal is to explain near- death experience phenomena within a framework of acceptable scientific principles.

According to yogi master Pramahansa Yogananda, miracles, religious, and spiritual experiences will soon be understood. He claims that while they seem to violate the law of nature they actually do not, and in the future these miraculous phenomena will all be explainable.

"In order to more fully understand this reality, we must take into account other dimensions of a broader reality."

John A. Wheeler

CHAPTER 3

PROFOUND JOURNEYS

**"Death is nothing else but going home to God,
the bond of love will be unbroken for all eternity."**
Mother Teresa

NDErs report impressions of time slowing down to what seems like eternity. In these cases, the experience of time seems to swell into an infinite expanse. It is often described as feeling as if you are one with eternity, having complete awareness, and enjoying total freedom. Many transcendental experiences also involve an expansion of consciousness beyond the way we ordinarily perceive the time-space continuum. In the metaphysical state of the NDE, people gain a much higher perspective of the temporal nature of time and space and the eternal/infinite nature of the afterlife.

What we are considering in this chapter concerns the phenomenon in which multiple individuals simultaneously know what others around them are experiencing while communicating via telepathy during the event. However, we're adding a switch to the "normal" way in which this type of communication and connection happens. We are focusing on shared and group communication from the physical dimension to the spiritual dimension, and back. The few reports that describe occurrences of this type of phenomenon are nothing short of astonishing. Beings connecting to the other side speak about clear and instantaneous telepathic communication. They talk about sharing similar visions, while consciously knowing what others are thinking, feeling, and perceiving.

Group NDEs, in which more than one individual experiences death in the same event, space and time, are slightly different from a shared death experience. In a shared death experience, a subject dies and someone who is nearby is aware of what is happening and may even observe some of the events that the individual experiences. Even though these can be considered two different types of metaphysical phenomena, we are discussing them together, because they both have to do with experiencing death, or coming close to it, or being nearby when death occurs and being pulled along for part of the ride, sharing the feeling simultaneously with one or more people.

Group NDEs are rare, but there are several that have occurred in recent times that are astounding. One tragic incident was reported by a man serving in Vietnam. He told of finding himself out of his body floating above the battlefield with several others, including the severely wounded captain in charge, all of whom had just died. They were all moving away from him towards a magnetic light in the distance, encouraging him to come along, which he decided against. Then, he suddenly woke up on an operating table. Later, he discovered that the men he was with during that NDE had all died.

In another case, which occurred one day in 1989, an elite group of firefighters, called "Hotshots," were fighting a raging wilderness fire. The men and women, numbering around 40, had been dropped by helicopter on top of a hill with a 40-degree slope. As they worked their way down the steep hill, the wind suddenly changed direction and the trees in front of them exploded into flames. They attempted to use their fire-resistant aluminum blankets, but to no avail. Within seconds, the trees were totally engulfed in flames, and all of the oxygen was sucked away. One by one, each of the crew members suffocated to death, falling to the ground as they desperately tried to get to higher ground.

The boss of the crew, a man named Jake, remembers saying to himself, "This is it. I'm going to die." At that point, he looked down at his body, and all the noise, heat, and fear from the blazing inferno vanished. As he looked around, he saw all the other firefighters standing above their own bodies. After conversing for a moment with the others, a fantastically brilliant light caught his attention, and inside this light was Jake's deceased grandfather. His grandfather told Jake that he could choose whether or not to go back to his body, but that, if he chose to go back, he would not suffer any major ill effects from the fire.

At first Jake argued that he didn't want to leave that place of immense peace and tranquility, but eventually he decided to return. And sure enough, he did not suffer any after effects from the fire, though the actual return into his physical body after his time as a non-physical being was one of the most painful events of his life. The members of his crew, all of whom miraculously managed to live, were astonished at the similarity of their experiences, including, as was the case with Jake, the discomfort of returning to their bodies. Their tools had all melted, and yet none of the firefighters were seriously injured or killed. Jake remembered sensing a protective sphere around him that kept him safe. He and the other survivors continue to discuss the amazing events of this group NDE.

Another case occurring in 1971 was reported by *Vital Signs* in 2000, a publication of the International Association for Near-Death Studies (IANDS). In this incident, three people were simultaneously struck by lightning. May was 22 years-old when she and her cousin, James, and his close friend, Rashad, were cutting fodder together in a corn field. Late in the afternoon, a thunderstorm descended, and they hurried out of the field by way of a metal gate. As James opened the gate, May lost her balance; James reached out and grabbed one arm, while Rashad tried to steady her by grabbing the other. At that moment, a lightning bolt struck the fence and electrocuted all three of them.

A moment later, they found themselves in a large gloomy room with an extremely high ceiling and walls made of dark stone. Even though she felt she should be afraid, May said that she was at peace. One of the men commented that the place would be well-suited for King Arthur and the Knights of the Round Table. That's when they realized that they were all having the exact same thought.

In fact, they felt completely connected in mind and spirit. Conscious of the others' thoughts, May felt that she knew both of them better than she had ever known anyone else in her life. They noticed that there was light coming into the chamber from an archway at one end of the room. This light was seen as a golden, embracing luminescence imbued with peace and contentment. Drawn towards the light, they passed through the archway into a beautiful valley, where everything shone with tiny sparkling bubbles drifting and floating everywhere. They quickly realized that each sparkling bubble was a human soul. To May, the realm was "heaven," her cousin saw it as a "gulf of souls," and Rashad described it as "Nirvana."

A light began gathering slowly at the end of the valley and out of the mist appeared a pure white being. Each member of this small group saw this figure differently: May saw it as a strong, female, Viking-like angel, the special angel who watched over May's family. Her cousin saw the same being as his late father, a career naval officer dressed in his uniform. And Rashad perceived the being to be the enlightened Lord Buddha. The being spoke to all three about things that would eventually come to fruition in each of their lives. May said, "We spent what seemed like an eternity in this place as we talked to our separate, yet joined entities." The being of light told all three that the hearts and souls of humanity would eventually be joined and that creed, race, and doctrine meant nothing. "No matter what we believed," said May, "we were all children joined under one God... We should treat all people as if they were a part of our soul because they were. All living things in the universe were connected to one another."

Eventually, they were told it was time to go back. They slowly drifted towards the archway, the pull becoming increasingly stronger until they were literally thrown back into the physical world. They floated there for a while, hovering over their bodies. May and her cousin felt as if they were on fire but fortunately weren't severely injured. Rashad had absorbed most of the shock and was severely burned. He spent several weeks in the hospital recovering and then returned to his home in India, where, about a year and a half after the incident, he returned to Nirvana. As James recovered from the lightning strike, doctors discovered that he had a brain tumor, and he died about three years later. May, who lived another thirty years, knew throughout her life that the connection that she shared with the two others is the same connection that we all share but usually fail to recognize in life.

Shared death experiences are rare, but there have been some striking incidents; for example, among hospice care workers who are often present at the moment when the person in their care makes the transition. At that moment, they describe feeling a "lifting" and seem to be able to sense the essence of the soul as it departs. In this way, they share in the dying person's experience, almost as if their own soul is connecting to the dying person's soul. They say often that they seem to be moving towards a light, and they feel momentarily enlightened by the event.

Not only hospice workers share in NDEs at the bedsides of dying people. After his many NDEs, Dannion Brinkley created Compassion in Action, the nation's largest hospice organization. He has been at the bedside of dying people over 300 times and says, "I have witnessed people lift from their bodies. I have seen what people would have called angels come and fill the room." As people fade into the afterlife, he has witnessed people talking to their deceased aunts, uncles, mothers, fathers, grandparents, and other relatives.

He has even had such a shared moment in his own family. "One of my greatest moments," he tells us, "was with my own mother. She was taking her last breath, after going through horrendous surgery, when she came back and said, 'Marian is here.' When my mother was 16, she had a 14 year-old sister named Marian, who was run over and killed." Apparently, Marian had come to take her home. Then his mother said, "I'm leaving now... Marian has come." Brinkley saw that she had turned to her right. He turned, too, and saw a radiant being standing there. His mother said, "I'm going. Don't let them hurt me anymore, and take care of your father."

In many cases, nurses and physicians will share the dying experience with their patients. Surveys have shown that over 30% of nurses feel strongly that they have psychically shared in their patients' deaths. In some of these incidents, nurses at home lying in bed will suddenly have the perception that a patient—often a "favorite" patient—has come to let them know that it's time for them to go, and they wanted to say goodbye. There have even been instances where the nurses will actually perceive their patient going towards a bright light. And, sure enough, in the morning, the nurse will call the hospital, only to be told that the patient has indeed passed on.

"Behold now the hope and desire to go back
to our own country, and to return to our former state.
How like it is to the moth with the light."

Leonardo Da Vinci

BLIND SIGHT

"The true promise of the NDE is not what it suggest about life after death, but what is says about how to live now".
Kenneth Ring

As we have seen, there are reports of people knowing exactly what occurred in an operating room when they were unconscious, and knowing peoples' thoughts and feelings during the time when they were clinically dead. There are also stories of people who have journeyed to the other side and found people there whom the visitors did not expect to see, because, to the best of their knowledge, these people were still living on the physical world.

However, when the visitors returned from these journeys and are asked about this confusion, they found out that, indeed, Uncle Joe or Aunt Betty or whomever had recently passed away. People have even found out that they are a twin during some NDEs, unbeknownst to them previously. It's common for people to see angels, gods, golden cities of light, and other celestial phenomena. So from the sheer numbers of people who report about NDEs and from the striking similarity of the stories they tell, it's hard not to accept the validity of NDEs.

However, there is still no definitive proof from a strictly scientific viewpoint. Is there a way to quantify the evidence of the soul from the NDE phenomena? In fact, there may well be some evidence, and it comes from an unexpected source: NDE stories reported by the blind.

The experiences of the blind are some of the most compelling in the field of NDE research. There are now several cases of well-documented blind near-death experiences (BNDE) on record. As with traditional NDEs, the blind journey toward the light, but they can see perfectly. They report lifting up out of their bodies and seeing the objects and people in the rooms where they are. In fact, there are now multiple accounts from visually impaired people stating that, during their NDE, their eyesight was "superior" to anything they had ever remembered or known.

What makes their reports even more amazing than those of traditional NDEs is, of course, that they normally *cannot* see. They often describe objects in the room where the NDE occurred. Many of these cases involve people who have been born blind, people who have never seen at all. Yet, when they were revived, they accurately described what instruments were used and the actions taken by the doctors. They tell of seeing their friends and relatives, describing how they appeared, and later had these descriptions confirmed as accurate. In another similarity with traditional NDErs, and for even more obvious reasons, blind subjects invariably do not want to go back into their bodies knowing that they will be blind again.

Raymond Moody reported a BNDE case in which an elderly woman, blind for most of her life, described medical instruments used and the color of the doctors' clothes immediately upon her resuscitation. There are several other incidents in which the blind speak about seeing medical procedures in the operating room from a high vantage point near the ceiling. Additionally, they report seeing the heavenly realm, beautifully colored landscapes, and cities of brilliant light.

In a BNDE case discussed by Kenneth Ring, Ph.D. co-author with Sharon Cooper, Ph.D. of *Mindsight: Near-Death and Out-of-Body Experiences in the Blind*, one blind person lucidly described the operating room and even went so far as to give accurate descriptions of the people in attendance. This blind person was also able to point out that the anesthesiologist was wearing mismatched socks, which was confirmed as true by the medical staff.

A classic example of a BNDE involves a man who had been blind since birth. At one point, his heart stopped for over four minutes. After he was revived, he had an astonishing story to tell. The first thing he remembered was floating up through the room and seeing what he perceived as his lifeless body lying on the bed. He also saw his blind roommate leave the room to get help. Then he remembers passing through the roof, emerging above the building, and discovering that he could see his surroundings quite clearly, though he had never to that point actually seen them. Ring and Cooper describe this ability as not optical sight but more as a kind of "transcendental awareness," which is what they refer to "mindsight." As they describe it, subjects see in detail, sometimes from all angles at once, with everything in clear focus, resulting in a sense of completely "knowing" every aspect of what they are looking at.

In all other aspects, this man had a traditional NDE, including passing through a tunnel, standing in a field where everything was bathed in and penetrated by light, hearing voices singing beautiful music in a language he had never heard, and finally being told by a loving being that he needed to return to his life. The things that he "saw," through "mindsight," make the experience unique.

Extensive studies conducted by Ring and Cooper convinced them that the BNDE reports are not fundamentally different from those described by people with sight. Their visual perception closely resembles traditional NDE, in that they see the radiant light, otherworldly landscapes, angels, and deceased relatives.

One case they presented, also a clear example of a shared NDE, involved a woman having an afternoon nap. In her slumber, she found herself projected into her stepfather's room at the hospital. She distinctly heard the nurse say, "He's going to go." Then she telepathically heard her stepfather say, "I give up." At that point, she became aware of two male spirit entities, who escorted him away. After the experience, she immediately called the hospital and confirmed that he was gone. She also confirmed the nurse's name, which she had heard during her out-of-body experience (OBE).

> **"Research strongly indicates
> that there is no separation in consciousness."**
> *Russell Targ*

"Who looks outside, dreams; who looks inside, awakes."

Carl Jung

On his website, near-death.com, Kevin Williams tells of a NDE that is "perhaps the most transcendental NDE ever documented."

It occurred in 1982 to a man named Mellen-Thomas Benedict, an artist working in stained glass who contracted cancer and was not expected to live more than six to eight months. One particular day, while under hospice care, he awoke very early, knowing that this was the day he would die. He called his friends to say goodbye, told the hospice worker what would be happening, and asked for his body to be left alone for at least six hours after his death. Then he went back to sleep.

The next thing he knew, Benedict began having an experience that appeared to be a typical near-death experience. However, two things set Benedict's experience apart from the usual NDE. Firstly, he did not come "near" death; he actually died. When the caregiver found him, he was already dead—she had no idea for how long—and, following his instructions, she stayed with his body for 90 minutes before anyone else arrived to resuscitate him.

The second aspect of his experience that sets it apart from the ordinary NDE is that he asked question after question to the light beings he met, and learned everything there was to know, from the time before the Big Bang to where the planet was headed over the next 400 years. As his experience was ending, he asked to be able to remember all "the revelations and the feelings" he had learned on the other side and was given a "yes" which felt, he said, "like a kiss to my soul."

What Benedict did differently that allowed for all of this knowledge was he simply asked for it. As he approached the light, which was similar to what he'd heard others experienced in a NDE, he felt it draw him towards it and he realized instinctively that if he went to it, he would be dead. So he said, "Please wait a minute, just hold on a second here, I want to think about this; I would like to talk to you before I go." And that was all it took: the experience was halted and he was allowed to have a number of conversations that filled his soul with knowledge and completely eradicated the deep depression that he had been living with for years; depression caused not from his illness, but from the poisoned, toxic, hopeless state of the planet.

Benedict explains: "You are indeed in control of your near-death experience. You are not on a roller coaster ride." This is powerful information for us to have. One of the first questions he asked was for clarification on "the reality of the situation." He was made to understand—through a kind of telepathic communication—that he would receive answers that conformed to his view of the world so that they would make sense to him, which he could then examine. He notes that everyone has this opportunity but—and this is well worth paying attention to—most people do not take advantage of it.

The insights that Benedict received during his visit to the other side were profound. The reader is strongly advised to read the entire transcript of that visit, which Benedict has shared on the website. But there remain several other important points that made an impression upon him, which I would like to mention.

First, Benedict became aware of the one-ness and connection of all life. Here's how he tells it: "As the light revealed itself to me, I became aware that what I was really seeing was our Higher Self matrix... It's also a conduit to the source; each one of us comes directly, as a direct experience from the source. We all have a higher self, or an oversoul part of our being. It revealed itself to me in its truest energy form... [It] is a direct connection to the source that each and every one of us has. We are directly connected to the source."

Benedict understood that we are all aspects of the same being and not in any way committed to one religion. He felt this "Soul Matrix" was the most overwhelming love anyone could every want; he was bathing in waves of curing, healing, and regenerating fields of love energy. He saw this soul matrix as a grid around the planet of which we are all part. And that our higher-larger-bigger self-soul is, in fact, dimensionally connected with it forever.

Before this incident, Benedict had grave concerns about mounting environmental issues on the planet. He felt humans were cancerous organisms to the planet. In fact, he felt that his extreme pessimism about life on Earth was what had poisoned his system and given him cancer. In his words, "That is what killed me. Be careful what your world view is." But after seeing the higher self matrix, after understanding that God is in each of us, in the light that we are made up of and in the vast spaces in between, Benedict's perception of humanity had radically changed. Now he could see our existence from a higher dimension and knew how creative, powerful and wondrous humans really are. "I did not know how beautiful we are."

He clearly felt after his NDE that life was awesome at all levels, high or low. He was astonished to see that there were no evil souls, and, of course, he questioned this. The answer was that no soul was inherently evil. The terrible things that happened to people might make them do evil things, but their souls were not evil. What all people seek, what sustains them, is love. What distorts people is a lack of love.

Revelations continued to flow through the light. Benedict asked, "Does this mean that humanity will be saved?" At that point a massive burst of explosive loving light energy pulsed through the matrix and answered, "Remember this and never forget, you save, redeem and heal yourself. You are always here, you always will be. You were created with the power to do so from before the beginning of the world." He thanks the light with totality, realizing we have already been saved. Feeling huge love and appreciation, at that point he experienced an enormous stream of light.

He then asked what the stream of light he just experienced was, and the light responded, "This is the RIVER OF LIFE. Drink from this manna water to your heart's content." So Benedict did this and exclaims, "I was in ecstasy." The light knew everything about him (past, present, and future) and all that he had ever perceived. The light then asked him if he had any desires. He whispered that he wanted to see the rest of the universe, beyond the solar system, beyond human illusion. Then he merged with the stream, going down a tunnel of light, experiencing what he described as soft sonic booms. He was quickly moving away from the planet, whizzing by the solar system and the galaxy, realizing that the universe is teaming with life.

Moving through an expanding fractal wave of energy, he realized his consciousness was taking it all in, like a child in Wonderland, seeing all of creation. A second light appeared, carrying those velvety sonic booms again, and he began perceiving what he describes as a holographic universe that he was interfacing. Then he found himself in a profound stillness (the void). "I could see or perceive forever, beyond infinity," he says. He felt he had transcended time, beyond the Big Bang, he felt he was one with the Absolute. He could see, hear, and feel the energy the solar system generates, realizing each system generates its own unique matrix of light, sound, and vibratory energy— its own personal identity.

> **"We are literally God exploring God's Self, in an infinite Dance of Life."**
> *Mellen-Thomas Benedict*

Truly, Benedict seemed to have moved into another dimensional realm of conscious existence, with a heightened and extremely accelerated level of perception. He had gotten to the end, outside of time and space, realizing that the source (God) is exploring the infinite through us. He realized that each of us is in the center of our own universe.

When an astronomer peers out into space in its an ever expanding universe, every object and star is moving further away in every direction from that center point. The actual perception of a person using the telescope is seeing them self at the center of that expansion. Even in another galaxy it would sill appear the same.

We are all co-existing within our own perceivable viewpoint. That was the point I got in watching William Arntz's film; *What The Bleep...* Are each of us at the center our our own universe?

> **"Yet there is no centre to the expansion; it is the same everywhere. The Big Bang should not be visualized as an ordinary explosion. The universe is not expanding out from a centre into space; rather, the whole universe is expanding and it is doing so equally at all places, as far as we can tell."**
> *Philip Gibbs*

The light made it clear, in new understanding that there is no death, that we are immortal beings, and that we have already been alive forever. Benedict realized that humanity was part of a natural living system that just recycles itself endlessly. He reached a point wherein he felt all of his questions had been answered. Benedict says, "Every human has a different life and set of questions to explore. Some of our questions are universal, but each of us is exploring this thing we call life in our own unique way. So is every other form of life, from mountains to every leaf on every tree... Because it all contributes to the Big Picture."

"Death is about life, not about heaven."
Mellen-Thomas Benedict

When the experience ended, he expected to be reincarnated and end up in a new life in a baby's body. However, to his surprise, when he opened his eyes he was back in the room, where the hospice nurse said he had been dead long enough for his body to begin to stiffen. For the next few months as he recovered, Benedict was in awe about what had happened. He often felt out of place, asking himself, "Am I alive?" This world seemed more like a dream than the other place. He noticed, though, a clear transition in his personality. "I could see nothing wrong with any human being I had ever seen," he said. "Before that I was really judgmental. I thought a lot of people were really screwed up... in fact I thought that everybody was screwed up but me. But I got clear on all that."

Three months later, the doctor looked at the before and after images of his disease and said the cancer was completely gone, claiming it was a case of spontaneous remission. To Benedict's surprise the doctor seemed very unimpressed. On the other hand, Benedict was certain this was a miracle, and he *was* impressed, "even if no one else was."

Benedict senses that the world has reached the optimum range in energy to cause a shift in consciousness, thus creating changes in politics, money, and energy. He believes that we are multidimensional beings and points out that one way to reach this higher realm is through lucid dreaming. He also says that, although humans are a speck on the planet, they are, unabashedly, legendary throughout the cosmos. As he puts it, "One of the things that we are legendary for is dreaming. We are legendary dreamers. In fact, the whole cosmos has been looking for the meaning of life, the meaning of it all. And it was the little dreamer who came up with the best answer ever. We dreamed it up. So dreams are important."

It seems as if Benedict really did see the light, and he is now in the light therapy business. His post death experience prompted in-depth insight that spawned interesting concepts and innovations, as well. One of his inventions involves the use of red light therapy technology. This invention uses biophotonic communication to accelerate natural processes on injured, damaged, or aging cells, by increasing their energy. This type of technology has been used on astronauts by NASA since 2000. Even though it's not widely known yet, the Department of Defense, the United States Military, Medical Doctors, and Naturopathic Practitioners are using this technology. Surprisingly, this advanced technology is now becoming available from manufactures such as LuxWaves in the U.S.A. Meditech in Canada and Thor in Europe for clinical applications.

**"No matter whether we are screwed up or not,
it is a blessing to be on the planet, right here where we are."**
Mellen-Thomas Benedict

**"The highest form of ignorance is when you
reject something you don't know anything about."**

Wayne Dyer

Many uninformed people continue to believe that NDEs are really just hallucinations. However, as has been thoroughly documented in this book, this assertion simply doesn't hold up against the voluminous evidence to the contrary. One NDEr, such as Alexa Hartung, points out how people recall the tiniest details of their NDE and even compare them with others, corroborating testimonies down to the smallest detail. Most significantly, hallucinations do not result in the same life transformative effect that NDEs often do.

Smokers, for instance, will quit cold turkey, and alcoholics will stop drinking. People who have had a NDE will almost always become much more spiritually inclined. In many cases, people have been miraculously healed of dreaded diseases after an NDE. There are several cases where people who have been extremely cruel to others and then have experienced a NDE have undergone such a radical transformation of consciousness that they became very friendly and compassionate towards others, even ending up devoting a goodly portion of their lives to the care of others.

In other words, a complete change in lifestyle, jobs, friends, emotional patterns, and overall personality and attitude is quite common after a NDE. Unfortunately, some of the drugs that doctors administer for surgery greatly impair people from remembering what happened, and that limits their ability to be transformed by their NDE later on.

Dr. Bruce Grayson, a University of Virginia professor of psychiatry, got involved in NDE after reading *Life After Life* in 1975. This book was written by Raymond Moody about the NDE phenomena. Eventually, Grayson met and began working with Moody, and they birthed an organization dedicated to this field. IANDS publishes a peer-reviewed scholarly journal, a member newsletter, and sponsors' conferences.

Grayson has been a major contributor, not only in the field of NDE but also in garnering greater respect within academia for this phenomena. Over the years, he has contributed to chapters in a number of textbooks in the fields of psychiatry and transpersonal psychology. He points out that the NDE can, from a strictly psychiatric viewpoint, look like a mental illness. Grayson says, "It's mainly because the things they [NDErs] talk about are so divergent from ordinary reality." People who have NDEs typically talk about leaving their bodies, hearing voices, seeing angels, etc. To the psychiatrically-trained eye, these things sound superficially like mental illness. However, psychiatry is prone to seeing things from a very materialistic and reductionist perspective.

Skeptics have not fully addressed all the evidence out there. Some compare the NDE with what we experience during lucid dreaming, or believe it the anesthetic, also claiming peoples' brains release a potent cocktail of bio-chemicals that create a hallucinogenic effect. Jeff Long M.D., a radiation oncologist and author of *Evidence of the Afterlife: The Science of Near-Death Experiences*, asserts that many critics of the NDE will believe that the experience was caused by hypoxia, which is a drop in the blood oxygen level. There is no strictly scientific, chemical, or medical explanation that explains how consciousness can exist apart from the physical body, while that body is clinically "dead" (i.e., no heartbeat or brain activity registering).

"Experiencers don't come back and believe that they've had an hypoxic or brain chemistry event. They know damn good and well that their consciousness separated from their bodies, and that is what the reality of NDE consists of."
Jeff Long

Another of the arguments posited to explain NDEs is that they are nothing but the bio-chemical reaction of a dying brain, a kind of psychological and physiological defense mechanism the brain undergoes against its own demise. While these arguments continue to remain the hypothesis *du jour*, none of them contain any hard irrefutable data supporting them, nor has anyone been able to design a double-blind study to test them. The data we do have supports the idea that these experiences are not just the effects of bio-chemicals or the brain's psychological escape mechanism. Says Long, "Most of the bio-chemical effects produced in the brain through strong electrical shocks, powerful pharmaceutical drugs, or sleep deprivation usually generate frightening, idiosyncratic hallucinations. They're certainly not the peaceful, transformative, and spiritually uplifting experiences of the NDE. Furthermore, these short-lived hallucinations usually *don't* radically change peoples' entire personality and lives but rather are an intensely-experienced, disorienting bombardment of images that often have no greater relevance or meaning to the one experiencing them. On the other hand, NDEs profoundly change peoples' values, attitudes, belief systems, lifestyle, etc. in ways that are embodied long after the experience is over."

"Our scientific power has outrun our spiritual power."
Martin Luther King Jr.

Melvin Morse, M.D., author of several books on NDE phenomena thinks that the $2 billion spent annually in the United States on the last few remaining days of a patient's life is completely unnecessary. "This money doesn't prolong life one second. Why do we do this?" he asks. According to Morse, there have been numerous studies that concluded there is very poor communication between patients, family members, and attending physicians, who are unable to speak "realistically" about the dying process. The American Medical Association (AMA) has stated that poor communication, along with our paralyzing fear of death, has directly led to the overuse of medical technology, which is dehumanizing, spiritually degrading, and extremely expensive to the family members expected to pay for it. Morse feels that there needs to be much more dialogue about the process of corporeal death and the soul's transition, focusing on its spiritual aspects.

Psychiatrist and psychotherapist, Stanislav Grof, also saw parallels to this basic sentiment about the dehumanizing and degrading effect of modern medicine. He says that,

> "Contemporary medicine is a slave to technical procedures and overspecialized body-mechanics and has forgotten the holistic aspect of real healing. Its conception of dying is dominated by the effort to overcome and postpone death at any price. Fighting for the mechanical prolongation of life, the quality of the patient's last days, and his psychic and spiritual longings do not receive enough attention. We see the tendency to shut out the old and dying people from family and daily life and to pack them off to nursing

homes and hospitals..."

When people in hospitals experience a NDE and attempt to explain what they saw to nurses and doctors, they are usually dismissed or patronized. They'll often get responses such as, "That's very interesting, but you are very ill," or, "That drug you were given often causes people to have strange dreams." Sometimes they are told, "If you continue to talk about this, a psychiatrist will be called in." This attitude within the medical field should change. Medical professionals need to become better educated about this subject and how to handle these kinds of situations.

"Truth is always stranger than fiction."
Lord George Gordon Byron

Pamela Kircher M.D., a hospice physician and author of *Love Is the Link: A Hospice Doctor Shares Her Experience of Near-Death and Dying* (2013), has ideas on how to integrate this immense quantity of data into the current medical curriculum. She believes that the first and second year of medical school would be the appropriate time to include it. It is certainly greatly needed to help the public deal with "end of life" issues. Hearing NDE stories can be enormously helpful for people missing their loved ones. Kircher feels that more medical literature dealing with this data needs to be published in reputable medical journals. Only then will doctors begin to pay more serious attention to the material and incorporate it into their practice.

This kind of education should extend beyond the current reductionist confines of Western medical beliefs to support these people at this critical juncture, immediately following a NDE. Unfortunately, most of Western civilization shows little interest or regard for the dying experience, offering no real psychological support and often doing quite a bit of psychological harm. Recently, organizations such as Compassion in Action [See Appendix B] and the International Association for Near Death Studies (IANDS) [See Appendix A] have spearheaded NDE assistance for experiencers, support for people grieving their lost loved and host certified hospice and medical training programs.

Currently, we are at a point in our society where we should begin to re-evaluate how we handle the dying process beyond our typical childish reactions of fear and denial. Clearly, Morse is not alone in his belief that we need to learn how to develop a new spiritual vocabulary for our society so that doctors, nurses, and patients alike can feel comfortable speaking about this inevitability with grace, wisdom, and dignity. As it stands, for all our sophisticated pretensions and scientific knowledge, we don't speak openly, honestly, or even intelligently about death or the afterlife. Instead, we prefer to live in a state of denial or superstition, clinging to religion and abject fear. Near-death studies and experiences have contributed significantly to a much more holistic and mature approach to the dying process.

> **"The sheer volume of evidence for survival after death is so immense that to ignore it is like standing at the foot of Mount Everest and insisting that you cannot see the mountain."**
>
> *Colin Wilson*

"Not only does God play dice, but...he sometimes throws them where they cannot be seen."
Stephen Hawking

A *US News and World Report* poll taken in 1997 estimated that, at the time, there were some 15 million NDErs in the US alone. Medical education covers things such as hospice and "end of life" issues, but oddly doesn't touch upon the NDE. Many doctors and nurses have been exposed to this phenomenon but simply don't know how to respond properly.

Despite this cognitive dissidence on the part of secular scientists and medical professionals, we now have incidences of complete 180-degree reversals from some of these same doctors and medical professionals who have themselves undergone the radical transformations resulting from a NDE.

One such doctor, Eben Alexander M.D. has written books about his experiences and his post-NDE awakening of consciousness. The book, *Proof of Heaven: A Neurosurgeon's Near-Death Experience and Journey in the Afterlife* (2012), became an instant best seller. The day of the naysayers are coming to an end and a new renaissance of spiritual truth and enlightenment is being ushered in. The enthusiastic response to Alexander's book is proof of this.

Initially Alexander, as a neurologist, didn't believe that consciousness survived after death. However, that was before he himself slipped into a meningitis-induced coma that lasted for a week. During that time, he had an NDE, which gave him the chance to see his soul's true nature and subsequently turned his worldview inside out. He now feels privileged to know that life doesn't end at the point of bodily death. He's gotten his peers scratching their heads.

"The place I went to was real in a way that makes the life we are living here and now completely dreamlike by comparison."
Eben Alexander

He saw that our temporal earthly journey is actually a very small part of a much bigger continuum in the infinite expanse of life. He described his journey as a grand tour of the largely invisible, spiritual side of our existence. His book is filled with powerful metaphysical descriptions and illuminating anecdotes about his profound NDE and subsequent revelations. At one point, he claims that, "The conscious brain blocks out the larger spiritual picture, just as the sun blocks out the stars from view." On the other side, he was connected with angelic beings of wisdom. Some of them appeared as transparent orbs glowing with loving light. He says all communication on the other side is telepathic. His senses and feelings were synesthesia-like and often omni-directional.

Alexander feels that pure, unadulterated consciousness originates from a higher spiritual dimension. By manifesting thoughts of love and compassion, we create the building blocks of which the spiritual realm is composed. Consciousness, according to Alexander, is the substrate of all reality. It's actually *more real* than what we call physical existence, which is conscious energy resonating at a slow vibration.

He was shown that, "Evil is a necessity because, without it, our free will wouldn't exist. Without the potential for evil, there can be no growth, no forward movement. As horrible as evil seems to be in our world, the larger picture reveals how love always ultimately prevails in the end and that we're better for having suffered through it." Alexander points out how humanity is facing a crucial time in its existence. "We need to recover more of that spiritual knowledge, while living here on earth," he says, emphasizing the importance of love and acceptance as a practice of daily life, and that we are a part of eternity. He believes that without recovering that memory of our larger connectedness and the unconditional love of our creator, we will always feel lost here on Earth.

"The physical aspect of the universe is a tiny speck of dust compared to the invisible and spiritual part."

Eben Alexander

SPONTANEOUS HEALING

"Reality is merely an illusion, albeit a very persistent one."
Albert Einstein

NDE reports are full of amazing and fascinating details, providing lessons that beam with profundity. But here is one that is unique even among traditional NDE reports. It is told in the book, *Dying to Be Me: My Journey from Cancer, to Near Death, to True Healing*, by Anita Moorijani.

Moorijani worked in the corporate world for some time before she was diagnosed with stage IV Hodgkin's lymphoma in 2002. For four years, she waged a fierce battle against cancer, but finally, in 2006, she knew there was nothing she could do to stop the devastating spread of the disease, so she decided to relinquish control over her life.

As soon as she had made this decision, her health quickly declined and she fell into a coma and was rushed to the hospital. The doctors had warned her family that she only had hours remaining, and that they needed to begin saying their goodbyes. It was while she was in this coma, which lasted for 24 hours, that she had her NDE. She reported afterward that she had experienced what life was genuinely about, and was not only aware of her physical surroundings in the hospital but also aware of the auspicious and omniscient other side of the soul's existence. Moorijani not only experienced a spontaneous healing as a result of her NDE, she also learned what the true meaning of existence was really about.

"A miracle is not the breaking of physical laws, but rather represents laws which are incomprehensible to us."
G. I. Guirdjieff

Even though she was unconscious, Moorijani was aware of her family members and doctors in the room with her. She reported later that she heard doctors outside her room discussing her case, even though the door was closed shut. One of the doctors said to his colleague that he felt there was no use in continuing treatment since the patient's organs had shut down, and it was obvious that she was in the process of dying. Later, after she had awakened from the coma,

Moorijani told her brother what she had heard. He became very upset that her physician had been so willing to dismiss fighting for her life. Ultimately, he located this doctor and brought him into Moorijani's room to confront him on the matter. Needless to say, the doctor was confounded by the fact that she had heard his conversation and emphatically apologized to her for the things he had said in that hallway while she was in a coma.

While Moorijani was on the other side, she experienced the deepest, most incalculable absolute love that she had ever felt in her life. She was aware of her family mourning by her side, yet describes how she felt amazingly alive and exhilarated, and wanted to share with them how well she was actually doing and that they did not need to feel sad. During her heavenly journey, she was visited by her best friend who had passed away due to cancer, along with her father who had died many years before.

> **"I knew that was really the only purpose of life: to be our self, live our truth, and be the love that we are."**
> *Anita Moorijani*

Moorijani perceived her eternal existence and describes it as a tapestry revealing a multitude of threads that illustrated other lives she has experienced before, and choices she had yet to make. She says, "I could feel my attachment to the scene receding as I began to realize that everything was perfect and going according to plan in the greater tapestry." She inexplicably understood that we have all had what are considered past lives; however, she realized that these lives are actually happening simultaneously. In other words, she understood that the concept of time was merely a concept that our human minds have conjured up because it is nearly impossible for a human being to understand the true actuality. She explains that with the way our minds work, there is no other way to assimilate the concept of timelessness without delineating it with past, present, and future tenses.

Moorijani became aware that her older brother was on a plane, hoping to arrive in time to see her before she died, and she found that she could feel what he was feeling, how worried he was that he would not be able to say goodbye to his sister. In regards to this empathetic oneness she felt with him and others whom she saw in a similar way during her NDE, she says, "It was as though their emotions were mine. It was as though I became them." She also became aware that she and her brother had been involved in simultaneous lifetime where she was his older sister and cared for him greatly as her younger brother. Furthermore, she knew that if she was going to pass away, her husband would quickly follow, too, since their souls' paths were purposely and divinely intertwined.

Regarding her cancer, innately understood that it was the *fear* of getting cancer that caused her cancer. She had seen her best friend suffer terribly with an aggressive disease, despite the best medical treatments in the world, and became incessantly fearful that she, too, would also develop cancer. Moorijani's brother-in-law had passed away from cancer, as well. She had an insight that all illness is first created on an energetic level; she understood that everything that happens to us only happens to us because we first bring it into our space energetically. She says, "Cancer is just a word that creates fear. Forget about that word, and let's just focus on balancing your body. All illnesses are just symptoms of imbalance. No illness can remain when your entire system is in balance." For instance, things like poverty, sickness, and relational hardships are things that only manifest in our lives if we hold these images in our energy fields. Adversely, the same results apply to those who bring positive things like loving relationships, prosperity, and good health into our energy fields.

Moorijani had experienced a plethora of miraculous and divine know-ingness of pure, undiluted truth during her NDE. She suddenly became aware of her father and best friend informing her that she had gone as far as she could in this heavenly experience, and that if she continued, it would be too late for her to go back. Moorijani knew that it was not time for her to die, yet she was also reluctant to return to her sick body and leave behind all the bliss she had found and embraced on the other side. She was then made aware that, if she decided to go back, she would quickly and completely be healed of her cancer and this recuperation would occur in mere days of her return.

Immediately after Moorijani's NDE, her cancer began to quickly fade away. During the NDE, she had been shown that she had a very long life ahead of her and that part of her purpose in coming back was so she could help others live their lives truthfully and fearlessly.

This parallels the stories of both Benedict and Alexander whose illnesses went into similar spontaneous remission following their NDEs.

Moorijani said, "I perceived that I wouldn't have to go out and search for what I was supposed to do—it would unfold before me." And it did. She explains that the paramount lessons she learned on the other side were the importance of loving oneself and consistently engaging in activities that bring us the greatest states of happiness possible, because feelings of love and joy are the underpinnings of our existence. She says, "I can't say this strongly enough, but our feelings about ourselves are actually the most important barometer for determining the condition of our lives!"

Once we see our true connection to the source, it becomes clear and logical that our thoughts, beliefs, and intentions can alter the physical universe. Using this knowledge to heal our bodies, as Moorijani has done, is the first step in this process; the physical matter all around us is next. her book tells us so much about our awesome connection to source, its magnificence, and its power.

If we are working and thinking in the highest order, can "noticeable" miracles and supernatural occurrences happen? These stories prove that what these people experienced had a direct effect on biological physical matter, thus responding to the change of belief and connection to the source that in turn creates miracles. It seems when we live in sync with the source, things do magically manifest for us.

> **"If you change the way you look at things,**
> **the things you look at change."**
> *Wayne Dyer*

CHAPTER 4
CONNECTIONS TO CONSCIOUSNESS

**"From the light we have come
and to the light we all shall return."**
Josiane Antonette

Some people have memories of a place before this life. The interesting part is that across the board, their stories speak of a very similar place. This is a place of light and love which they must exit to come here. Reports of pre-birth memory occur occasionally after a person has a near-death experience, as if latent memory from the spirit realm retained through the birth into the physical plane is jarred loose by the NDE. Some elements in the pre-birth reports show clear parallels to elements in the NDEs.

People talk about being in a different time and space dimension, in the presence of a great light, and feeling great reluctance to leave that heavenly realm, as if the spirit were second guessing itself, or needing a nudge to go back into earthly existence and face the challenges of another round.

Anyone familiar with NDE phenomena has heard these types of statements in cases of people reluctant about coming back to life. These correspondences provide a segue into similar other types of spiritually transformative events.

Pre-Conception Memories

**"Birth in the physical is death in the spiritual.
Death in the physical is the birth in the spiritual."**

Edgar Cayce

In ancient times, as well as in contemporary eras, people who have had these beyond-physical experiences say that it is as if they were home *before* they were born into this physical plane. They seem to agree that the nonphysical plane they inhabit before they are born is their true home. We leave that home as traveling souls, coming and going within this infinite universe.

In this section of the book, we will look at reports that have been shared by people preceding, during, and immediately after the birth experience.

In some cases, after an NDE, people claim to have clear memories of their childhood, memories they thought they had long since forgotten. Some even claim that the NDE unlocks memories of being in the womb. Though it is rare, a few people state that they receive a glimpse of memories prior to their conception. Such people may, for example, report that they remember being in situations where they chose the parents to whom they would be born. These types of cases confer ideas beyond the normal, linear, and mental constructs or frameworks that we usually associate with our memories.

Some people, experiencing the prior life review, say that life begins at the moment of conception. Others, however, maintain that the soul doesn't fully enter the body until the first breath is taken. Still, others have memories of traveling to earth as a being of light and entering the womb at the moment the sperm meets the egg. Within milliseconds of that moment, they *choose* things like their hair and eye color, bodily size, physical attributes... all the genetic material available to them. For others, even though they may not remember choosing such things, they may suddenly understand why they were born with a debilitating disease, handicap, or hardship as they pass through a life review.

If you were to spend some time reading accounts of such pre-birth experiences, as I have, you will find that evidence abounds showing that a baby's soul not only remembers the experience of being in the womb, but also remembers its mother's words and thoughts during the pregnancy. There are cases wherein the baby's soul actually meets its mother's soul in advance of its conception. Taking this a step further, some remember the beautiful time spent in the heavenly realm before being born into the earthly plane. This reminds us of one old wives tale: the crying of babies is because they are upset about being away from heaven, their pre-birth home.

Relatively few people have written about pre-birth/pre-conception memories. Most of these stories are scattered throughout the course of history. Ian Stevenson M.D. considered to be the grandfather of modern metaphysical research, is one of the few scholars to have done studies and written books about this and other related phenomena. He interviewed children who remember their life in heaven and incarnations prior to their birth. These children are too young to contrive these stories. There have been cases in which children claim to know who murdered them in their previous lifetime.

"At our core, each one of us is an eternal light being who temporarily masquerades as one of the actors on the earthly stage."
The Carmens

Up until recently, no one had shed so much light about people's memories prior to their birth than Elizabeth and Neil Carman in their co-authored book, *The Cosmic Cradle*. The Carmans document numerous cases of pre-life memories in the heavenly realms, where souls are given certain choices about parents, their life plans, and what they call "cosmic contracts." Through their extensive research, the Carmans discovered a wealth of information from stories from numerous cultures, religions, and traditions about the existence of memories prior to birth.

They compiled all these pre-birth stories, ranging from thousands of years ago to the present, derived from almost every culture on earth. Ancient Greek and Roman philosophers spoke and wrote about how human beings had prior lives. They describe how we were once in a perfect state, traversing holy mountains and meadows, free from disease and pain. Zen Buddhism teaches that, prior to birth, a being is shown the karmic entanglements and the different lessons that will need to be worked through. The soul is then shown the lifetime that will best serve the purpose of releasing as much karma as possible.

According to the Carmans, many other religions, including Christianity, Judaism, Islam, Mormonism, and a host of tribal religions, refer to pre-life existence. In fact, most ancient and tribal religions believed in pre-life existence, and, unlike larger mainstream religions, those groups did not lose the concept after entering the modern world.

The Carmans note that pre-life doctrine was removed from the Christian religion around 300 A.D., along with other Gnostic texts. The Carmans feel that recently, materialistic thinking has dominated the media and education systems, influencing an individual's perception into upholding values that are less important in the bigger picture.

In their extensive research, the Carmans found many parallels between NDE and pre-life experiences. During the pre-life or "in-between experience", some individuals recall coming to Earth through a tunnel into their mother's womb. The Carmans found references in philosophical and religious texts to the tunnel, and a kind of two-lane highway of souls.

The story of *The Cosmic Cradle* itself is very interesting. When the book was first released in 2000, it was a 760-page encyclopedia of pre-birth/conception data. When the Carmans connected with a new publisher, they were asked to reduce it in order to reach a wider audience: the revised edition, which appeared in 2013, is slightly more than half the size, at 392 pages. I have read both books, and I find the new shorter version does as excellent a job as the longer one did in conveying the extensive information the Carmans have gathered.

In 2001, I attended a convention of the International Association for Near-Death Studies (IANDS) in Seattle, where I met the Carmans. I was fascinated by their work and invited them to do an interview with me. For many years, I have been interviewing people who can provide insight on topics such as NDEs, and in most cases the interviews last just under an hour. However, with the Carmans, six hours passed by when Elizabeth was finally dragging Neil out by the arm.

In a somewhat bizarre coincidence, after I recently moved, I found out that I live only a few miles away from where the couple makes their home, so I have had several more opportunities to discuss their work with them.

The information the Carmans uncovered and compiled—and shared with me in that remarkable interview—is so interesting and empowering. I believe the information they have accumulated, organized, and published has the ability to reshape public perception and the potential to shift people's awareness to a better understanding of who we really are. They corroborate a basic fundamental understanding that we have been here before, and we will be here again. Their work presents a strong case that we are part of an infinite source, we are eternal beings, and our consciousness continues forever.

Here are some of the common elements that the Carmans uncovered in their research about existence in planes other than the physical one in which we inhabit:

- The heavenly world is people's true realm
- There is limitless love in the heavenly world
- There are soul groups of which we are a part
- Heaven is teeming with souls
- Telepathy is the mode of communication in non-physical realms
- There are divine planners, groups of spirits, angels, and guides
- Souls are allowed to preview lives and choose among them options for parents and life lessons
- Some souls are reluctant to be born, while others have a strong desire to receive a body
- People with pre-life memories have no fear of death

These elements appeared continuously, reported from people all around the world and of all ages. In cases in which a parent communicates with a child to be, there seems to be a pattern. In some cases these incoming souls manifest in the form of a sphere, bubble, or light, always to the parents' surprise.

Summarizing this aspect of their extensive research, the Carmans say that the human soul is generally seen to be a luminous spark or sphere of light, sometimes with a radiant electric blue hue, which can manifest as tiny orbs or balls of light, or as bubbles that can be sparkling, pearlescent, or of a liquid golden sheen. Indigenous tribes of North America also saw the soul in a similar way, as a spark of illumination, an element of light, or a miniature star. Some medieval Christians saw the soul as a glassy spherical vessel that exited the body as light.

"Pre-birth memories transport us beyond the materialistic idea that heredity and social environments explain human life."

The Carmans

The Carmans feel strongly that we come to this earthly stage with a preexisting script. But we forget that script, and our earthly desires tend to divert us from the path of love we ambitiously chose before diving into life, inevitably altering our course. In addition to our own scripts, their research shows that family links are enduring. The souls of ancestors take interest in new births connected to their genetic lineage, in some cases acting as guides or guardians of the newly arriving spirits and others as guides back into the Soul Matrix.

Again and again, these children that have deeper memories will say how they have come from the light. These children refer to being somewhere else before they got here, and about moving through time and space, making their descent into matter. Some have stunning memories of descending down a tube or tunnel to Earth as a blissful light moving at light speed, into a vortex of creation, some even encountering the duality of light and dark. According to the Carmans, a four-year-old named Derek said, "Mommy, I was a star in the universe waiting for you and daddy to become my parents."

Children with these memories often talk about places of pure light and about missing that heavenly land from which they came. They talk about how beautiful it is there, and show no fear of going back to be in heaven—essentially, of dying—to their parents' grave concern.

The Carmans explain that it is as if each of us has a cosmic contract. A soul's goal is to be born into a happy home, to families of healthy, happy people, where it can obtain spiritual growth and fulfillment. These choices are not based on economic or material satisfaction.

Note, too, that this idea of pre-life planning can be found in ancient texts going all the way back to Plato. Ancient Gnostic texts tell us that Jesus picked his disciples in heaven before he took a human form here on earth.

The Cosmic Cradle is filled with stories of the choices made by particular souls who are considering manifesting into a physical body. In a fair number of cases, the soul doesn't want to be born into the physical. For example, in one instance, a soul was enjoying hanging out, being in a dimension of joy, peace, and light. But once it understood that there were other souls, compadres, friends, and that it would be possible to re-connect with on the other side, the soul was reassured, and the choice to come into human form was easy. Furthermore, according to the Carmans, souls communicate with each other about the timing when they decide to jump into physical bodies, so they can be together in a given lifetime.

> **"Souls face a paradox:**
> **Remain in an ideal world, or opt for a challenge."**
> *The Carmans*

My thought is this: Maybe beings in that *other side* dimension perceive time differently than us living here. Time seems to be non-linear in the heavenly matrix realm, but, from what I have gathered, it is not completely nonexistent.

Another interesting point from the Carmans' work concerns the evolution of souls. They found that souls have varying levels of maturity. The more-evolved soul has greater freedom to choose, much like a graduate student, and, perhaps for that reason, the more mature souls pre-select their life plans more wisely. However, it is not, as some believe, simply that each successful lifetime elevates the soul to a higher (and less troublesome) plane. Nobody learns when things are easy. Sometimes a being needs to learn a lesson that requires selecting an unfortunate experience in order to progress to the next point in their spiritual development.

> **"Even the most advanced souls accept a lower position**
> **to help fill in the gaps of what they need to learn."**
> *The Carmans*

The graduate souls seem to have personalities that are wise and compassionate, wherein the new students sometimes dabble in destructive and manipulative patterns. This group will possibly waste lifetimes relearning the same lessons. Unconsciously knowing only struggle is their ability to maximize the manifestation of love in their life.

There are many stories of people's lucid memories surrounding the actual moment of a soul's conception in the physical realm. The concept of a soul glimpsing the sexual union of its conception is not a new idea. This idea is written about in the *Tibetan Book of the Dead*, and both Buddhist writings and the Kabala mention the image of the incoming soul perceiving a great deal during love-making that leads to conception.

In some cases, a child will eventually confirm things that occurred, specific events that had taken place, which he or she had no way of knowing but indeed saw from another plane of existence. In many cases, children never mention it to their parents until they were older or mature enough to discuss it, sometimes decades later.

Spiritually gifted parents have reported subtle awareness of an incoming soul when the child is conceived. People have claimed to have seen a pillar of light during lovemaking, and lights of different sorts, only afterwards finding out that that was the event when their child was conceived.

> **"Youngsters who recalled not so much**
> **other planets as multidimensional realms..."**
> *P.M.H. Atwater*

One of the persons the Carmans interviewed had very profound memories and insight, stating, and here I am paraphrasing, "how every being was linked with the entire megaverse, with infinite growth potential." When reading their book, and retrospectively thinking about other material, I began to detect an underlying tone of other possible planetary options for souls. Some information seemed to indicate incarnations on other planets, and in many cases people referred to Earth as the dense planet or spoke of being on "the planet" as if there were others to choose from. .M.H. 'sstudies, based on

93

thousands of interviews, uncovered surprising statistics including that 20% of adults identified with being from another planet. Within a children's study, based on several hundred interviews, only 9% identified with being from another planet. But they identified with being from another dimension at a rate of 39%.

Spheres made of the light seem to be an ongoing theme throughout this book. Other researchers besides the Carmans have made similar observations, including Pastor Howard Storm who wrote about his NDE, and P.M.H. Atwater, both reported seeing millions of light spheres. There is an ocean of consciousness out there, and those who have sailed in it seem to agree that our souls have a spherical shape. This makes sense, given that so many of these reports involve passing through a tunnel of one sort or another.

To give a better idea of the kinds of experiences the Carmans uncovered as they investigated pre-birth awareness, let's look at a few specific interviews included in their book.

A 70-year-old retired military intelligence officer recalled being on what felt like a high ledge overlooking the earth with an entire assembly of souls. (Note that coming to an edge in space, or being on a cloud looking down on the beautiful blue sphere of Earth, ready to make the leap into the unknown, are common threads in stories of pre-birth communication, along with seeing a descending stairway, tube, or spiral leading to birth into the physical realm). As he stood there on that ledge, he overheard conversations around him of people surveying the earth and deciding on their future parents. His guide gave him several choices of parents. As soon as he made his decision, he felt himself entering a huge tunnel at fantastic speed, following what he described as a ribbon of light down the long, spinning tunnel.

Similar to what was reported in the typical NDE, people who experience pre-birth memories mention dialogues with celestial guides or guardian angels. Only instead of discussing whether or not to return to the physical life, the discussions centered on to whom they would be born, and sometimes even which other beings in the heavenly realms they wished to rejoin in their upcoming lives.

"We are explorers who come to earth as a cosmic

> **spark or consciousness from a higher source. . . .**
> **Everything emerges from the absolute field of**
> **pure existence and ultimately returns to it."**
>
> *The Carmans*

Another woman had pre-life memories activated by an NDE that occurred when she was eight years old. At that early point of her life, she claimed to recall around thirty different lifetimes, and not just the lifetimes but also the time in-between the lives. In her words: "I saw all of my costumes. I remember coming from all that is…and pushed out like a projectile of light."

Another woman interviewed by the Carmans, Beverly Anderson, recalls being in the heavenly worlds and working things out with her angels. In planning her next life on Earth, she became very hard on herself. She felt that she didn't do a very good job in her previous life. She pointed out the areas she needed to work on, and her angels asked, "What do you want to do better?" She replied, "Well, I don't know. Do you have any suggestions?" In the next moment, she was given a choice of life scripts. She said it was "like going to the movies in heaven." She was given three or four movies she could choose from and was able to choose everything, even the time, culture, ethnicity, country, and economic circumstances of her next life. Beverly said, "If one is really paying close enough attention to their choice of scripts, they can cook up a real interesting movie."

One of the most amazing stories told to me by the Carmans concerned a man named Glen and his pre-birth recollections. Glen had a detailed memory of his entire pre-birth period, in which he was shown three different sets of couples to choose from as parents. The first couple he was shown were very rich. His guide indicated that if he chose that couple as his parents his life would be very easy, but, in the end, he wouldn't feel rewarded or fulfilled. The second couple he was shown were in the bedroom, actually engaging in sex at that moment. This couple was financially secure but not wealthy. Finally, he saw a third couple, and he was told by his guide that they were poor. If he picked this set of parents, his life would be filled with many trials and tribulations, and he might not reach his full potential. Glen then asked his guide, "If I choose this couple, with whom my life will be the most difficult, will my reward be the greatest in the end?" The guide answered, "Yes." According to Glen, when he chose that third couple, the guide asked him twice if this was really the life he wanted to live. Glen responded it was.

Glen even remembers the night of his conception, seeing his young mother turning around in the car and looking at his sister, still a baby, sleeping in the back seat. He also remembers music playing, the car door being open, and his parents having sex, which ultimately resulted in his conception and birth. As a young child, Glen became curious about what he remembered and asked if he had been "created by mommy and daddy in a car". His mother responded with, "We don't talk about things like that." So, he didn't talk about it again until he was twenty five years old. He again let his parents know that he was intrigued by a memory and wanted to verify if it was true. He asked them if they could remember when he was conceived. They exclaimed, "That was 25 years ago! How could we possibly remember that?!" Glen replied, "What if I could supply some of the details?" His mother asked her husband if he had been talking to Glen. The father insisted that he had not, saying, "You know I wouldn't talk to him about things like that!" Glen went right ahead and described the details of that amorous night, the make and model of their 1929 automobile, as well as other intimate details. His parents looked at each other in amazement and in unison said, "Yes, that's how it happened". Both parents were simultaneously stunned and quite embarrassed that he had witnessed his own conception.

Elizabeth Carman makes an interesting observation about pre-birth memories. She isn't sure whether it is true that every individual chooses his or her future life path. She feels that perhaps some people, depending on their level of consciousness, have more freedom to choose than others. She sums it up by saying that, in the case of someone like Buddha, an incarnation offers nearly unlimited possibilities. On the other hand, someone else, who might be considered to be in the kindergarten stage of consciousness, has far fewer options to choose from. But, someday, that soul will arrive at the graduate school level, and they'll have more options, as well as the necessary remedial course requirements.

Neil Carman, too, has a fascinating and somewhat controversial theory that our long-term memory comes from outside of the physical matrix. Science dictates that memories are created with a brain cells by the thoughts people think after birth. Neuroscientists have long been trying to isolate memories, both short and long-term, within specific brain cells. However, he believes something different. As he puts it, "Our pre-birth [i.e., long-term] memories come from a place before there was any connection with so-called material existence." Thus, says Neil, long-term memory might be connected to the root of consciousness itself and not dependent on the brain at all.

The ideas presented in their book serve as reminders of our true nature, urging us to learn how to follow our heart. We need to know that we are truly spiritual beings, and this physical existence is just a temporal abode. We are cosmic voyagers of the light, who come here to experience the physical dimension with all of its many challenges. When we leave this plane, we carry our character strengths and virtues with us into our next soul journey. Many people are unconsciously homesick for that heavenly home, and this spiritual longing can cause a sense of loneliness, alienation, and despondency.

I hope this information will inspire people to search within themselves and reignite their higher self, because it is truly our divine birthright to remember who we really are. After all, humanity has been operating on outdated thinking and repressive ideologies for a very long time. The time has come for us to see the truth and live in the freedom of understanding. The information becoming available can help guide us into this new millennium with clarity and fulfillment.

> **"A rational man can... believe in reincarnation on the basis of evidence rather than simply on the basis of religious doctrine or cultural tradition."**
> Ian Stevenson

PRE-INCARNATION COMMUNICATION

Pre-birth experiences are giving us a glimpse of the life we lived before this one, the life our unborn children are living now — the life before life.
Sarah Hinze

On occasion you will hear a story about a mother communicating with her fetus during pregnancy, and to most people, that doesn't sound farfetched. But when someone speaks about communicating with an unborn baby prior to conception, it seems like a stretch. It sounds more believable when a mother says she dreamt about seeing and conversing with her child to be. In some native cultures, dreaming about babies is a natural prophetic process for a woman prior to conception, and for a long time has been part of ancient religious beliefs. In many aboriginal communities in Australia, the conception of a child is defined as a spiritual event during which the "spirit-child" selects its parents.

Some information in this new field of research is coming via siblings, grandparents, adoptive parents, relatives, and friends of the spirit "to-be" as well as the future parents, who most commonly report a sense of connection with the spirit of the coming child. The message sometimes comes through a dream, intuitive perception, inner voice, vision, hovering presence, a light, or the occurrence of synchronistic mystical events. Although this doesn't occur in every pregnancy, if parents are attentive and tuned-in or consciously open to reception, such perceptions of contact happens. Sometimes such visionary experiences can actually be validated by the child as it grows up and begins to speak of what it remembers, though such validation may take years. But in Western culture, many women are reluctant to share their stories, because these kinds of experiences are not readily accepted.

What's important to realize is that an individual has been touched by another conscious being – an unborn soul. The evidence is established simply by the sheer number of people who have reported a sense of having had some experience of communication with their future child. When these baby souls reach out directly, connecting to their future parents, in most cases women, will commonly report having a paranormal experience. Is it occurring because of the mother's psychic power, or is it the baby's psychic abilities that allow it to reach from beyond? And if the baby is sending signals prior to conception, then is the baby spirit communicating from another dimension?

There are only a handful of published authors on this topic. These authors receive continued gratitude from the individuals who were able to share their stories. These women were amazed and shocked to find that so many other moms had similar experiences. Women say it's very freeing to find out that it has occurred to others, and that they are now able to come out of the closet about it. I'm personally thankful to those authors as well, for assembling, writing, and publishing this information. It gives me a better outlook and understanding about the "here-after," or rather, the "here-before."

In addition to the Carmans, a number of other authors have presented clear-cut cases of pre-birth communication. Among these is Stevenson, author of the book *Spontaneous Pre-Birth Recall*. Another is Sarah Hinze, whose book *We Lived in Heaven*, is subtitled, "Spiritual Accounts of Souls Coming to Earth" and provides many stories of families who had contact with the souls of their as-yet-unborn children. Another is Walter Makichen, author of *Spirit Babies*.

These writers' field of interest could very well be the most important area of spiritual research at the forefront of major metaphysical breakthroughs.

When it comes to digging below the surface on this topic, a researcher named Elisabeth Hallett has unearthed some amazing stories. While working on a book about postpartum events, she noticed an unexpected pattern. Mothers kept mentioning that they felt the connection to their baby begin long before their baby's birth, and in some cases prior to its conception. She discovered that not only do mothers have pre-conception communication from babies, but also in some cases, when the baby becomes a child and is able to talk, he or she recollects memories occurring around the time of their conception. While many of these children seemed to have lost these memories over time, she discovered, to her amazement, that some of the children retained memories from this "other place" throughout their entire lives.

Hallett is the author of several books and has a background in nursing and psychology. The book she released that caught my attention is called *Stories of the Unborn Soul: The Mystery and Delight of Pre-Birth Communication*. This book takes the reader on an awe-inspiring journey into an amazing phenomenon. Hallett set in motion a way to look at human conception with new eyes.

My own pre-conception experience was the subtle kind. It happened over and over during the months before I conceived my daughter.
Elisabeth Hallett

Hallett's book reveals patterns that I believe begin to define a hidden language between these birthing souls and their mother to be. Though every story is individual and unique, each has a similar point of reference, a theme, making it relevant to other mothers' similar experiences. Among these reoccurring themes or patterns are the following:

- Human beings are souls before conception
- There is communication with future parents prior to conception
- Parental interaction prior to birth occurs (at a subconscious level)
- Humans participate in an agreement before taking physical form
- Souls as spirit babies can and do announce their arrival
- Babies' souls have the power to make their presence known
- Spirit babies encourage parental procreation
- Children speak of siblings prior to their conception/birth
- Parents are told names
- Parents are given requests to help with conception and pregnancy
- Ancestors/relatives act as guardian angels to help baby spirits be born
- These guardian ancestors also manifest in pre-mortal visions
- Children claim to know people in their current family from prior lives
- Reluctant souls can miscarry, but they often return later

- Random, profound, loving incidents can bring souls together later
- Souls have a tendency to incarnate together in families over generations

From what I have found, these people have received a gift, in a sense, by knowing a bit about from where they come, and where they will be again someday. Moreover, what people have seen prior to conception gives the rest of us a glimpse of the other side, of another dimension of which we all are part.

I noticed from Hallett's book that, after people were told by medical professionals that they could not give birth, it was especially surprising to them when messages from a baby spirit occurred, and doubly surprising when conception of that baby actually happened. On the other side of the coin, people using birth control and ignoring the dreams or signs of a coming baby were shocked when pregnancy occurred despite the precautions against it. These souls are coming through, and they seem to be letting people know in advance, especially individuals who will end up being the most surprised!

Another point that Hallett makes is that hypnosis, which is often used for a number of reasons during pregnancy, can allow mothers to communicate with their babies' spirits at a deep and subconscious level. For example, a mother under hypnosis can go back to different points during her pregnancy and discover that the baby picked up every single one of her thoughts and emotions via telepathy. Hypnosis helps reach into an individual's subconscious and, in some cases, brings up lost and distant memories, on occasion activating transcended states.

Sometimes baby communications during pregnancy occur in the other direction, i.e., from the baby to the mother. Such communications can serve as messages to parents about the baby's health or biological needs. In one case presented by Hallett, an expectant mother's friend had a dream. In that dream, the baby told her mother to eat more protein. At her next visit to the doctor, the expectant mother's blood work showed she needed more protein to alleviate her high blood pressure.

Sometimes during psychic readings, people will receive information about baby souls. Of course, information that comes through psychic readers is not definitive. But some of the information received in this way does match up with other stories coming from many other sources of pre-birth data.

The "baby spirit whisperer" of psychics, the clairvoyantly gifted Walter Makichen, brought forward extensive data about what is going on at this entry door to life. I've found examples of incidents where mothers claimed psychic readers were accurate at knowing the number of future children, their genders, and the approximate times in the mothers' lives the births would take place. Psychics commonly report seeing these unborn souls as a form of light in someone's energy field. Even when the psychics and the medical sonograms were incorrect about gender, sometimes the parents' that had received visions were still on target.

Like psychics, some women have a natural state of heightened awareness and can more easily sense the loving vibration of these baby-souls-to-be. Meditating is a good way for a mother to achieve this heightened awareness and become more in tune with her baby; in fact, baby souls will often come to people through meditation. Motivated souls can be very persistent, almost pushy, when trying to incarnate. Women sometimes perceive it as if the baby spirit has its suitcase all packed up and ready to go! And it's not just the mom; dads too, on occasion, will receive messages, seeing a baby or small child in his dreams, and the dreams occur more frequently as conception is nearing.

It is reported that these baby souls come to parents asking if it's okay to be their baby. These souls indicate that it is okay if it doesn't work out, as there are more back-ups and alternative plans to easily manifest elsewhere. But there also seems to be an astral waiting line behind specific parents or mothers. We could ask the question: Are parents with exemplary sets of beliefs and values necessary for a soul's optimum growth, and are they in demand?

Using meditation during an unwanted pregnancy can be a tool for the mother and father to communicate with the spirit baby, letting the soul know that it will not have a good home, physically or emotionally, at that particular time. It has been found that spontaneous mis-carriage can follow after affectionately assuring the child soul it had nothing to do with it, lovingly urging it to find another mother, and gracefully convincing it that there was a misunderstanding about con-ception. This will naturally motivate the soul to find another mom, or wait until the opportunity is right with this mom. It seems a fetus soul has the ability to traverse between dimensions, wandering between the heavenly place they come from and the earthly place where we live. They like to know at birth that "it's on" – 100% full-time living – for another round of life.

It also seems baby souls like to nudge this process along, like little cherubs or cupid angels, encouraging conception. Some couples believe their unborn child actually had a hand in bringing them together. If these souls are like us, then we don't need to communicate in a childish manner when consciously reaching out to them. In one of Hallett's cases, the baby soul specifically told the parent not to use baby talk! "I'm an evolved soul and appreciate being talked to in an adult manner."

Grandparents or great-grandparents will appear in the form of guardian or angelic helpers through dreams. Sometimes the mother does not re-cognize them as relatives. Then later, when looking at old photographs of ancestors, she might recognize the younger image of them and real-ize at that moment that it was the grandparent or great-grandparent with their future child in the dream or vision. This also occurs from the other direction, wherein the child at a young age will say that a grandparent (whom they had never known) escorted them to here from heaven, much to the surprise of their parents. When parents show their child pictures of the grandparents, the response is sometimes, "No, not them". But similarly, once the photographs of the much younger grandparent come out, the child will recognize them.

Similarly to what had been portrayed in the recent book and movie, *Heaven Is for Real*. People are said to see their elders not looking as old when they have a spiritual vision or get a glimpse of the other side. Therefore, souls seem to appear in their prime, at their most vibrant age. It is almost as if the soul consciousness is projecting or using a holographic representation to converse during cross-dimensional communication.

Sometimes, as we've seen, intuitive, accurate information about a baby will show up in a vision or dream. For example, a soul will come through, perhaps to a sibling, expressing its ambivalence about being a baby again, and shortly thereafter the mother miscarries. It seems quite likely that jumping into life to become a mortal might be a bit scary for some. However, all is not lost. It is thought that in cases of miscarriage, abortion, or sudden infant death (SID), these souls will eventually come back, often to the same mothers, to be born later in time. In cases of the early death of a young one, say through SID, those same souls can be welcomed back into the fold through birth to a relative. This suggests that an agreement with our parents is what gets us here, usually at a subconscious level. There are also other much bigger hands at work behind the scenes that allow this total miracle to take place.

Keeping religion intact through the ages has been critically important, because it has kept a basic language of spirituality intact. It has truly brought us the ABCs of a spirit dialect, and without it we would have no context or dialogue to grow from—no reference point. Just imagine: without the words "soul," "spirit," and "heaven," how would we explain any of the concepts presented in this book?

"Our language is the reflection of ourselves."
Cesar Chavez

Is it time to develop a new language that communicates to future baby souls with conscious intention? If so, this new language needs to be a language that is seen (visual), not just words or thoughts, but iconic scenes and imagery. It cannot just be the sound of a word but rather, a picture – after all, a picture is worth a thousand words. From my observations, a new or expanded spiritual language needs to be created in order to initiate a cross-dimensional communication between baby spirits and their parents-to-be. Could this understanding help future generations grow spiritually and help the evolution of humanity?

"...their hearts changed as powerful evidence
their eternal nature reveals to them a new paradigm
regarding the sanctity of each human life."
Sarah Hinze

When I try to qualify metaphysical occurrences I look for patterns, and when similar stories are repeated continually from several people, I start to think that there is something to it, something warranting further investigation.

The daunting task of quantifying metaphysics becomes easier when a pattern becomes clear. When that pattern also follows a thread that runs through other transformational experiences, similar to what I have assembled for this project, it gets my attention. Upon reviewing the material, it made sense to include it in this book, even though it steps a bit outside my original research protocol.

In this book I purposely and primarily focused on ordinary people who had experienced some type of transformative spiritual experience, or people who had experienced profound memories prior to conception. I also focused on information from the hypnotic regression and induced after death communication field; in these cases, people are stunned and deeply affected by what they had experienced. I avoided information from people claiming to be psychics and mediums, those who attempt to channel a deity of some sort, as well as chemical or electrically induced supernatural experience.

That being said, in this next section, I have provided information about one man who clearly seems to have an intuitive gift. His transformative information is so similar to the thread explored throughout the book that it's presented below.

> **"Spirit Babies come... with specific needs**
> **vital to the fulfillment of their destiny."**
> *Walter Makichen*

My discovery began through a set of interesting circumstances. I once met a woman who ended up leading me to Walter Makichen's book about spirit babies. While we engaged in a normal conversation about the business at hand, I noticed something curious and had to inquire about it. She began telling me how she had tried to get pregnant for several years through the use of advanced medical means, with no apparent success, at least until a friend suggested that she read

Makichen's book *Spirit Babies*. Shortly after that, she conceived, and she strongly believed that Makichen's book had a definitive effect on her astounding conception. She ultimately bore a set of twins!

The way she explained it to me was that Makichen's book takes the reader on a magical mystery tour that clarifies the human spiritual journey into birth, the metaphysical undertones of the karmic manifestation of life, and its connection to the deep past. I was astounded for several reasons. First of all, while researching metaphysics I had never heard of this book. Secondly, I was surprised how similar the stories were to what I had been assembling for this book. As Makichen is a self proclaimed psychic, it's inclusion here is justified by what was reported by a third party.

The book was introduced to me by an individual who had had a successfully profound experience with it. And when I began reading Makichen's book, I realized it would be profound for me, too, because here before me was such a treasure trove of data that fit into place and filled in blanks to other material I had been assembling.

Walter Makichen died in 2011. Knowing this, I felt much more inclined to move his beautiful and unique insight forward, as far-out as it may be for some people to grasp.

> **"Perseverance in the knowledge of the Supreme Spirit… comes from knowledge of the truth"**
> *Ved Vyasa*

Throughout his life, Walter Makichen was a very motivated psychic. As a clairvoyant, Makichen discovered a powerful reoccurring pattern in the area in which he was best gifted. He claimed that when he was a child, people knew intuitively to ask him befuddling questions because he had insightful answers, and he also felt he had innately insightful abilities. But for many years, he gave little thought to his metaphysical talents. One day, however, while attending the University of California in Berkeley, he had a lucid vision that changed his career. After a set of bizarre paranormal experiences he decided to follow his intuition and became a professional psychic reader.

At some point in this career as a psychic, Makichen realized that he had a particular knack for connecting souls ready to come into this world—he called these souls "spirit babies"— with couples who were hoping to bring the gift of a child into their lives. By connecting with these souls, he was able to communicate important and sometimes critical information between the spirit baby and the potential mother or parent. The entire point of a spirit baby is to be born. It is propelled by the force of karmic laws to seek out parents and enter into a birth agreement, usually communicated at a subconscious level to its parents. Makichen was able to cross into another dimension and help people communicate with beings that didn't have a body yet, before they were born or even conceived. According to Makichen, this knowledge helped facilitate conception.

"Every spirit baby has its own beliefs about what kind of environment is necessary for its growth."
Walter Makichen

There is a section of Makichen's book entitled "Calling to Your Future Child: Learning to Communicate with Spirit Babies." The immediate question for most of us would be, "How can a baby possibly communicate?" Right off the top, he states that it's not as challenging as it seems. They are souls, like the rest of us, and most are seasoned travelers with all the nuances and complexities of the full grown human being they will become one day. Sometimes a mother's intuition can pick up information from their babies. Makichen was helpful in teaching his clients how to connect and communicate with the soul before it was even conceived.

The importance of communication on an spiritual level can be seen when emotional issues are found to hamper a couple's ability to get pregnant. He named this "karmic condition". The baby spirit's spiritual demeanor, disposition, and self-beliefs are also part of the dynamic spiritual agreement. This agreement is, at a subconscious level, what Makichen called the "conception contract".

Makichen worked to help couples with this conception process, many of whom had exhausted medical options and still weren't able to conceive. He was quite successful at creating a communication pathway to connect parents with their babies-to-be. Several ways he did this was by encouraging his clients to communicate through meditations, chants, and visualizations. He wrote meditation scripts for his clients, while reminding them to be aware of any possible telepathic, visual, emotional, and intuitive signal or messages.

Makichen had also begun to establish something in a broader scope. His talent was teaching people how to communicate to the Soul Matrix-Heaven, or at least the part of it where baby souls reside. It's as if he had begun to create a new language rooted in experiential glimpses of our higher self.

He was a pioneer in developing a new vocabulary used for inter-dimensional communication. This vocabulary helps people communicate with loving beings coming in from a different realm—beings who want to be here with us, as our future children.

"Conception is both spiritual and physical union."
Walter Makichen

Makichen said there were many cases in which he not only knew a baby's gender, but also its temperament and personality, confirmed in many cases years later by the parent. He claimed to perceive an in-depth psychic view at the karma behind the parents and the new soul incarnating, stating how these souls wanted the best opportunities to challenge themselves in situations wherein they would be confronted with issues in order to incur optimum spiritual growth. According to Makichen, a soul will choose to be with a particular individual based on some karmic condition. This is right in line with the theme that keeps being brought up by transformative event experiencers.

A common belief in some religions and now part of the New Age ideal is the concept of Karma. Karma is the force that connects people in order to fulfill their destinies. It is not limited by time or space, and involves unfinished issues. Makichen enlightened one client about this emotional blockage with becoming pregnant, and she was able to work through it. It took two years, during which she intensely practiced meditation, yoga, and positive self-affirmation. Through this process she was able to successfully conceive.

Makichen advised his clients to practice:

- Meditation
- Self-affirmation
- Yoga
- Chants (hymns/songs)
- Communication with the baby
- Paying close attention to dreams

He reports it is common for spirit babies to communicate through dreams. Sometimes these dreams reveal past life connections.

One of Makichen's clients was experiencing a recurring dream. In this dream, the client was fighting in a battle, holding a soldier as he took his last breath. She immediately woke up anxious and restless. During a clairvoyant reading, Makichen connected with the soul of the dead soldier. He noticed a scar on the soldier's cheek and listened as the man explained, "We were brothers in that lifetime, and I died in battle. It is time for us to be together again". When he relayed this information to his client, she was shocked that Makichen knew about the facial scar, because she had never told anyone about that part of the dream.

Makichen's explanation is that "past lives are often the source of present-time child-parent relationships... Friends, siblings, children, and parents often work out issues and lessons from other lifetimes by taking on parent/child roles in this one." But the conception ultimately comes down to an alignment to create the energy bond to form it, and an acknowledgment on the part of each participant that they have all forged a new karmic bond.

An agreement to manifest life is a commitment on the part of each participant to play a particular role in fulfilling each other's destiny. What Makichen call the conception agreement, sounds very similar to what the Carmans referred to the cosmic contract. Both are symbolic of the spirit's intention and commitment in taking on the challenges and lessons of life in the physical plane.

The prospect of this new identity can be frightening to the incoming soul. The conception agreement occurs at the parents' subconscious level, outside of this physical plane. Somehow, it never seems to be a perfect science; there are often misunderstandings and disagreements. When this happens, the spirit baby does not receive the reassurance it seeks and will hold back from the conception. Either the soul will hold back from being conceived, or, in cases when conception has already occurred and there is discord, the soul will leave and cause a miscarriage. Makichen's reports indicate that a soul in that situation will likely return at a later time, when things have been ironed out or when the setting or situation has changed.

> **"There are no mistakes, no coincidences.**
> **All events are blessings given to us to learn from."**
> *Elizabeth Kubler-Ross*

In some cases it seems that baby spirits need a certain gender or a healthy body in order to fulfill their destiny. One woman came to Makichen to solve a pregnancy problem. Makichen saw the soul wanting to be a boy, but the future mother's intentions were set on a girl. The karma of the soul that was supposed to incarnate was a boy. So at a subconscious level, there needed to be a meeting of the minds. As soon as Makichen conveyed the information to the couple, they immediately began putting loving and affectionate thoughts towards a baby boy. Within two months she became pregnant with a baby boy. This is one of many successful cases reported in Makichen's book.

Abortion is an issue that stirs a lot of emotions, for people on all sides of the issue. Whenever Makichen publicly lectured, the issue of abortion inevitably came up. His ideas on the issue provide us with a new way to look at it. He says that the non-physical dimensions have a different set of energy dynamics, and souls in that dimension are eternal. They continue their journey, even after an abortion. As he points out, "After an abortion the unborn spirit does not die, nor does it lose the ability to create." But Makichen points out that those souls can react very negatively to an abortion. They can feel disheveled, shorted or cheated, while others move right through the experience and show great compassion for the mother.

What Makichen understood is when a soul decides to incarnate, the spirit baby's consciousness is a mélange of memories and potential. All the accomplishments, failures, and significant events of the past lives swirl in the free-form state of the spirit oval. The soul goes through memories as a stream of consciousness with no particular direction, aware of its history and purpose. The force of karma draws the soul from this free-state into an identity that will enter into the lifetime that it will become. At this point, the soul makes its appearance into the energy field of a prospective parent. This means the soul is always preparing for its next incarnation, paying attention to its prospective parents' world. This is the time when parents can connect to spirit babies. Even if parents don't get their questions answered, according to Makichen, the communication helps the spirit baby access the information necessary to create its new identity.

Makichen always encouraged conception-wishing clients to pay close attention to their dreams in case their spirit baby was trying to send them messages. He suggested that they begin asking simple questions and saying things like, "I love you." He felt this kind of communication created a nurturing energy that supported the baby's growth. Here are several questions that he found would most quickly and efficiently elicit helpful responses:

- Have we known each other before?
- Why did you choose me as a parent?
- What is our karma together?
- What do you know of your destiny?

To those trying to conceive, he continually advised that parents should practice meditation, make frequent affirmations, and perform chants. Throughout his career, Makichen found that parents who followed these processes had more success conceiving. These processes help bring subconscious information into conscious awareness, thus encouraging spirit babies to manifest from the divine. Makichen helped many parents bring babies into their lives, and continues to do so through the influence of his book and other published materials.

I believe that Makichen's work in meditation and other mental and communication exercises is accurate. People can learn to intentionally communicate through this plane into a parallel dimension, and this can be the cornerstone of a new form of extra-dimensional communication.

"We live in an interconnected universe.
There is a web of energy that binds the spiritual andthe physical
worlds together in a harmonious union."

Walter Makichen

CHAPTER 5
TRANS-DIMENSIONAL THERAPY

**"Life between death and a new birth is as rich
and varied as life here between birth and death."**
Rudolf Steiner

With the recent discovery of the ways in which therapists can use hypnotic regression to take people to between-lives experiences, more professionals are looking at the value of this healing modality. And now there are other theraputic systems that are able to access deeply into the human psyche, accessing realms where space and time are experienced very differently than normal. Therapists are pulling deep, profound, and nearly unimaginable information from this inner/other dimensional subconsciousness data stream, which seems connected with our true home. The messages coming through this pipeline speak of love, spiritual growth, and other profound insights regarding humanity's quest to better itself – on earth and in the universe.

I believe the sooner we come to this understanding, the sooner we will evolve as a species, a race, a planet, and as players in the galactic community. From my research, it seems as if the heavens and advanced intelligences are watching. I believe we have an opportunity to shine as a powerful cosmic force in the universe. All we have to do is *see* who we really are, and what I call trans-dimensional therapy (TDT) can facilitate that.

The following information illustrates how, at our very core, we are pure love energy using this physical container for only one purpose—our spiritual growth. Living is a blind test. We have no instructions, no pre-preparation, no conscious idea or memory of what we are being tested for, but it remains the test of a lifetime, literally. There is no pass or fail grade; there is no grade at all. We score what we are supposed to score, which is determined by ourselves, and based on how much we want to spiritually grow and evolve. Each lifetime comprises a class, or a page in a very long book, a book with an infinite number of pages.

**"I did not begin when I was born... I have been growing,
developing through myriad of millenniums. . .
Incalculable times again shall I be born."**
Jack London

In this amazing field of between-lives regression, there are very few therapists publishing their cases to date. The earliest I found were Joe Fisher and Joel Whitten, M.D. Ph.D. in their 1988 book *Life Between Life,* followed by Michael Newton Ph.D. in 1994 with *Journey of Souls*. These authors should be considered the grandfathers of techniques in which I to refer as trans-dimensional therapy.

Newton, with several bestselling books under his belt, is now retired and only trains a handpicked few in this specialized field of psychotherapy. Newton has mentored many therapists, but at this point only one student stands out in my mind as the next leader in the exploration of this new, profound, and powerful field, Linda Backman Ph.D..

Backman was lucky enough to work personally with Newton to help him develop and manage his patient- and practitioner-training clinic. She has now released a book on her findings, after being involved with over 8,000 hypnotic regressions to date.

**"I no longer believe in reincarnation.
I know this is reality in which we live."**
Linda Backman

In her 2009 book, *Bringing Your Soul to Light: Healing Through Past Lives and the Time Between,* Backman displays a wealth of information on this amazing treatment phenomenon. Through regression hypnosis people are able to reach a particular level of consciousness, which she defines as a place where the soul exists at a pure energy level. She provides a clear impression that we exist within a multidimensional reality while traversing the physical reality.

In her practice, she helped people resolve interpersonal issues. But as a side effect, people *lose* the presupposition that there is nothing after life, very similar to the NDEr's side effect. This instantly frees them of any fear of death they might have had. Her clients come to understand:

1. Their souls' purpose
2. How their souls are connected to a soul group or family
3. They have known other souls they are connected to through multiple incarnations
4. The ways in which their past lives have affected their current ones
5. That fear and worry are not values of the soul

This form of regression therapy helps the individual discover the nature of their soul, providing them with information about the other side and what lies ahead. It enlightens them about their journey, often giving them insightful guidance about their current life and its purpose and progress.

> **"That every soul energy does indeed carry over from life to life [is] a phenomenon known as continuity of consciousness."**
> *Linda Backman*

In this regression therapy, she uses hypnotherapy techniques to bring clients back to a period between lives, when they existed as pure soul energy. During this process, they function simultaneously in the body and in the spiritual realm, processing in parallel with their higher selves, connecting with their deepest essence, as part of their eternal spirit. The in-between life therapy has a very cathartic effect on these clients.

Hypnotherapy is a powerful tool to successfully treat smoking, addiction, weight problems, low self-esteem, pain management, and other physical and emotional issues. Between-life regressions are a type of transpersonal treatment sometimes loosely referred to as "soul therapy" or Life Between Life Therapy (LBL). Backman points out that neither the client nor the therapist determines the depth of the experience. Interestingly enough, she says it's determined by the guides in the unseen world! The guides decide the content to be experienced during the regression, according to Backman. As one of her clients said, "The master allows me to see what is never-ending, the eternal energy of the source."

Backman says that in the heightened trans-dimensional state that occurs between lives, people begin to understand and experience who they are at a "core soul level". She reports that people are greeted by their spirit guides, "spirit buddies," greeters, angels, associated souls, and/or welcoming committees. Her clients have made statements like, "I'm glad to be back," sounding as though they feel that the spirit realm is their true home. These spirit buddies, who are perceived as light energy by Backman's clients, guide them into the divine realm and navigate their transition, helping them adjust to being home.

Clearly, there are similarities between the experiences of those entering the space between lives and those who have undergone NDEs: the presence of guides and the appearance of these guides as light energy, to name two. Another interesting parallel is that both for between-lives travelers and NDErs, the guides often choose to block out parts of their inter-life or NDE memories.

This has been the subject of debate at IANDS conventions. I had been leaning towards the idea that it was just impossible for the human brain in the physical existence to decompress the complexity of the experience, and that it was not information being "intentionally withheld". But based on Backman's reporting, I am being forced to revisit these ideas.

> **"God conceals from men the happiness**
> **of death that they may endure life."**
> *Lucan*

During their session, Backman's clients go through the death/reentry process as they enter into and then exit from some of the lives they previously lived. They view these transitions almost as holographs, as they "open the curtain" into memories and unlock emotions, thoughts, awareness, and associated energy blockages. As she puts it, people "simultaneously reap a positive, literal and energetic evolutionary change, a shift in perception."

During these therapy sessions, people are clearly operating from an altered state, a highly intellectual and intuitive level, while totally lucid about what is going on, functioning from an elevated perspective. For example, helping clients understand cruel or heinous events, with a soul-level explanation, allows them to access key scenes and events from a higher dimensional view point.

"The karmic benefits of regression therapy can be profound."
Linda Backman

In some cases, a client goes far enough to reach what Backman refers to as the spiritual "home room". She explains that each of us has a conglomerate of high-level souls intimately attached to us as teachers. This is a council of wise beings who provide us with support, direction, and loving acceptance. These beings will encourage us in difficult family and life situations that challenge our integrity, trust, and ability to use and explore the pure love energy to its highest and best order. In some cases, the elders nudge souls to go back to Earth. The question is: Are the elders pushing souls to do this in order to encourage personal spiritual development, or enhance humanity's growth? Or perhaps both?

Backman's clients universally report, upon returning from their journeys into the between-life space, that in their past lives (as is the case in their current lives) they dealt with all kinds of issues, including physical, emotional, and behavioral. Each lifetime seems to have a specific intention or reason, all having to do with situations that encourage spiritual growth.

"The overreaching purpose of our soul…is to progress as an individual soul and in gaining wisdom to enhance universal consciousness…our soul stems from the divine ineffable highest realm of energy, wisdom and love."
Linda Backman

Through her work, Backman has learned that, whether we are a man or a woman now, we all have experienced lives as the opposite sex. She believes that deep within the human consciousness we carry the archetype of both the male and female blueprint. She also states that there is a revolving theme around each soul on its path to bringing consciousness and light to the awareness of others, and emphasizes how crucial it is to heighten our collective vibratory energy. Each of us has the opportunity to enhance and transform ourselves and others around us.

117

Her understanding of what is important to learn from these journeys into the spiritual realm, while we are in this current existence, is that we need to focus on universal values, rather than our beliefs about money or sexuality. We should also focus on recognizing that we are all souls "advancing at the perfect speed for our journey at any point in time".

Many of the stories she tells from her sessions involve unusual or strange observations. For example, some clients spoke of past-life incarnations on other planets. Another client noted that she didn't like the existing veil that surrounds Earth, separating the spiritual realm. She feels that the fifth dimension is the realm of pure love. In her regressions, she reports some clients move beyond alpha states deeper into what's called the theta state, where that fifth dimension is experienced.

One of Backman's clients had yet another term for my definition of the Soul Matrix, calling it the "neural net". She said that the neural net is the nervous system of universal consciousness. It is a framework or grid that connects all of creation and manipulates space and matter from a multidimensional level of which souls are inherently a part. This client is not the only one who has been using these energy-related terms to describe the "energy matrix of the universe" lately. It's as if there is an astral geometric relationship between the spiritual realm and the physical universe.

"It is love, not religion, that creates spiritual growth."
Sandra Rogers

Meta-Consciousness

"I am more than any or all of the faces I have ever worn. Our essence is eternal and the only part of us that is real."
Beverly Anderson

Joe Fisher was a journalist for the *Toronto Sun* and metaphysical researcher whose curiosity led him to research and write *The Case for Reincarnation*. In the spring of 1982, as Fisher was researching the book, which would be published two years later, he connected with Joel Whitton, a neurologist and professor of psychology at a Toronto medical school. To help with the research on his book, Fisher tried to persuade Whitton to allow access to some of the latter's files. Whitton's unequivocal response was memorable: "I'm afraid I can't help you. I'm a respectable psychiatrist. I don't want be a lightning rod for the fundamentalist movement."

Despite that first unsuccessful meeting between the two, the situation was eventually turned upside down when, several years later, Whitton reached out to Fisher and invited him to co-author a book about the intermission souls take between lifetimes. Not surprisingly, Fisher, whose book was already published and doing well, debated working with Whitton after their previous brusque meeting.

Only when Whitton explained what his thirteen years of research studies had uncovered, was Fisher finally on board. The doctor had been using a technique he called hypno-regression, which allowed him to pull memories from his subjects of what happened to them between lifetimes. In 1988, Whitton and Fisher published their book *Life Between Lives,* which explored scientifically the void separating one incarnation from the next. It was the first Trans-Dimensional Therapy research of this kind on the planet.

Whitton had accidentally discovered his breakthrough therapy when he inadvertently changed his regression protocols during a past-life regression. He called this between-lifetime state "metaconsciousness." Later, Newton, who performed similar work, named it "super-consciousness", and this is the same state that Backman called the "transdimensional state". Recognition of this state predates all of these contemporary authors: In *The Book of the Dead*, Tibetan shamans refer to it as the "Bardo", wherein the Christians and Catholics refer to it as "purgatory".

Life Between Lives shows how we choose a specific karmic script for each incarnation and use it to supply the experiences we will need in that life for spiritual growth. In the larger picture, then, by choosing to live through the hardships of our lives, we are helping with the evolution of the human species as well as the universe's 'collective spirit'.

Whitton and Fisher provide many instances of between-lives regression, comparing them side-by-side with many ancient beliefs. These comparisons show undeniable parallels, providing evidence that such knowledge has been with humanity throughout the ages. And it's hard to accept as pure coincidence that the experiences related by Whitton and Fisher correlate almost word for word to the rebirth and near-death experiences that have been discussed earlier in this book.

In 1982, a Gallup poll determined that sixty-seven percent of Americans believe in life after death. In their book, Fisher and Whitton quoted Kenneth Ring, a well-known NDE researcher and author, who said that "what happens after the initial stages of death ... remains an open question." What the two authors hoped to achieve, after all these millennia, was to try to answer this basic question.

Whitton found through his early efforts in past-life regression that when he asked his subjects under hypnotic trance to go back to a time before this life, they could easily recount episodes from another time, another place, with great detail. He felt that under hypnosis, his subjects knew as much about those previous lives as they did about the life they were currently living on this physical plane.

As a neurologist, Whitton was aware that whenever his subjects brought up traumatic events from past-life memories and moved that information into their conscious awareness, the result was often a rapid and dramatic healing of the psychological problems they had been dealing with in their current physical lives. Though he himself could not explain why this happened, he found this past-life therapy was a highly effective method for healing in cases in which mainstream treatment had not achieved any appreciable improvement in patient condition.

Whitton felt obliged to state that there was no scientific proof that his clients were experiencing past lives, though both he and his subjects were convinced of its reality. He personally believed that the subconscious mind stores knowledge of former incarnations, and, like many of his colleagues in the field of psychology, he believed no thought or behavior is accidental. But unlike his colleagues, Whitton felt that the cause for behavior in some cases reaches back to a time prior to conception.

As he compiled data for his study, he found a common karmic thread. He discovered that souls tended to jump into incarnation to interact in ever-changing relationships with the same entities they had known before. In many cases, first-time subjects visiting the metaconscious dimension would be shocked and disoriented when they came back to normal consciousness, sometimes even unable to speak for several minutes. One of these subjects said something that might explain this intense confusion: "You have woken me up into an unreal world."

"Having filled our sights with the life to come, we plunge once more into the crucible of Earthly existence, where deeds determine destiny."

Joe Fisher

When the metaconscious state is reached during the session, the subjects usually find themselves standing just at the moment of death in a previous life. In other words, the memory/journey begins as one lifetime ends and moves directly into the period in which the subject immediately begins writing the "karmic script" for the next lifetime. The authors further point out that all cognitive emotions—love, guilt, ecstasy, anger, admiration, remorse, greed, loss, lust, dread—are held temporarily in the astral body, ready for evaluation, something each soul must face during its exodus from the physical, upon it entry back into the Soul Matrix.

The soul seems to focus on any emotional suffering that was inflicted on others in complete sensory detail, but these emotions will be felt as if they were being inflicted on the soul-self. Simultaneously, the soul realizes that the time for changing those attitudes and fixing those mistakes is gone forever—in that lifetime. In other words, the soul achieves a complete and precise accounting for who it once was and what it stood for. The spirit is then healed with radiant loving energy by souls of light that encourage it to learn from past mistakes.

One of Fisher's underlining messages seems to be that some spirits are so ashamed that they have trouble facing and embracing the beings of loving light. But shying away could lead to an undesirable fate. People who fail at the path set forth for them will have to re-challenge it again. For example, souls of suicide victims will be faced with similar circumstances and hopefully resist the temptation to take their own lives again in the next incarnation. They must permanently overcome it, or they could experience a vicious continuous cycle.

As souls, we set ourselves up for situations that we will eventually learn to master, overcoming a particular weakness. Some souls resist incarnation because of the nasty karmic condition they know they will have to face. However, they are shown that they must eventually return, at least to understand and balance out the pain they caused others. Thus we can see, from Whitton and Fisher's work, that committing bad acts in a physical lifetime retards spiritual progress, and requires a more difficult and intense learning environment, so as to move past the losses and take the next step.

Fisher explains that, "at stake is our personal integrity and inner morality," handicapped by our own wrongdoing. Out there in the metaconscious plane (aka Soul Matrix), everything is known, and the soul's consciousness feels pity and shame for committing horrendous acts against others. In many cases, they choose in a subsequent life to become a victim specifically of whatever harm they had inflicted in their previous lives. They learn that whenever they do negatively toward others, no matter how big or small, becomes part of their soul forever. As the Buddha said, "Karma is like the stream of time…It is never destroyed."

The implications of the life review makes me think justice in a new way…it is simply that we receive back what we have given out… measure for measure, perfectly, with no possibility of error."
Kenneth Ring

Therefore, each soul's task is to create a karmic balance in order to facilitate its spiritual growth, to learn right from wrong at a spiritual level, and to understand the effects of its actions in a larger context over many lifetimes. Observing karmic trends and patterns in this way helps the soul to gain the "big picture" of its existence within the universe. And, of course, the soul observes positive experiences as well, and knows that such actions lead to the soul's evolution, increasing the odds of species survival in the physical dimension. It is as if setting spiritual markers enhances survival for DNA in this physical existence so that souls will always have a place to perpetuate life .

The ultimate need is for spiritual "mutation" to help us remember what not to do, to encourage us to lead lives with higher ethical standards, and thus to ensure the continuity of life. In this way, we can continue, without destructive hindrance, to spread our life-giving, living DNA throughout the universe, giving souls more options to manifest in the flesh, to learn, evolve, and experience the physical plane for eternity.

One of Whitton's subjects stated, after many successful in-between life regressions: "I have been allowed the barest glimpse of the levels of creation, that are far above anything I can even begin to put into words. I was made to feel everything that we do has meaning at the highest level. Our sufferings are not random; they are merely part of an eternal plan more complex and awe-inspiring than we are capable of imagining."

Fisher uses a terrific metaphor in his book, which doubles as a perfect summary for this section: he says that it is as if we are artists who make rough sketches. Once incarnated, we set out to work on the intended masterpiece. After death, or through the metaconscious state, we are able to step back and view the work we created with our life. Mastery of living, like mastery of painting, demands repetition to learn what works and what does not.

> **"All our lives and inter-lives lie within that infinity, as do the karmic patterns [that] shape personal evolutionary development... Earth being no more than a very necessary testing ground conducive to spiritual evolution."**
>
> *Joe Fisher*

"The soul is an emanation of divinity, a part of the soul of the world, a ray from the source of light. It comes from without into the human body, as into a temporary abode... it wanders in ethereal regions, it returns to visit... it passes into other habitations."

Ralph Waldo Emerson

Hypnotherapy has been successfully used in inter/transpersonal healing and psychological growth. Hypnosis has been proven to tap into the subconscious mind. Its effectiveness can best be understood by its ability to bring repressed memories that have been buried deeply in the psyche to the surface. A typical hypnotherapist will use regression therapy with their patients to re-experience traumatic events from patients' lives. This is done in order to work through negative and often repressed memories that are causing some kind of neurosis or psychological pathology.

Occasionally, hypnotized subjects regress back into what appears to be past lives. In many cases, this leap comes as a surprise to the therapist. In these instances, subjects return from the hypnotic state claiming they were in a different body and time period. What is interesting is that many of these people possess uncannily accurate information about people, events, and geographical locations that can be verified historically and turn out to be accurate. This is usually information that they shouldn't, by any rational account, be able to know anything about.

More interesting, however, is what happens when people under hypnosis remember what they were doing "in-between" lifetimes. The similarity to the recollections of what NDErs see is uncanny. The correlation between those two phenomena creates a basic consensus, a template of what it is like on the other side. Through the NDE, we see information about what it is like to leave the body, whereas hypnotic regressions give us information about our "in-between" lives immediately after death and prior to conception. Each phenomenon corroborates and substantiates the other, giving greater credibility and legitimacy to all.

Fisher and Whitton passed on the "in-between lives" torch to Newton, although he came upon the phenomenon on his own, like Whitton.

Newton began his career as a psycho-therapist and counseling psychologist, with a specialty in hypnotherapy. Originally, he was very traditional in his approach, and only worked with people who were interested in trying to heal childhood trauma and resolve various psychological problems they had in their adult lives. People would sometimes ask him to help them with past-life regression work, and he would tell them, "No, I don't do that kind of work."

At one point, Newton met with a patient who came to him with a severe bout of loneliness and depression. Not having much luck with the session, out of frustration, he asked her to go to the source of her loneliness. Inadvertently, the word "group" came up, and it seemed to act as a trigger for her. Suddenly, she saw a soul group that she had known in-between lives but that was not part of her current life. She began crying, and said, "I see them all! They are now in front of me." The intensity of her reaction, and the relief of her symptoms that followed, was enough to convince Newton that his clients could benefit from bringing this type information to the surface.

> **"Death is nothing but a change of form."**
> *Swami Satchidananda*

From that case onward, he began incorporating "life between lives" therapy and past-life regressions into his practice. The results he saw in his patients were tremendous. Through this deep psychological healing, a patient could see "the self" as a soul; once this occurred, issues, hang-ups, and problems simply melted away. In some cases, he recorded a 180-degree shift in the person's attitude, resulting in significant changes to both perceptions and beliefs.

Naturally, Newton initially worried that people would think he had lost his marbles. But soon this became no concern. Today, his primary work is teaching practitioners how to help their clients learn about their immortal spirits and make them aware that, as he puts is, "we all have this within us". The memories are all there and only need to be recovered. He feels that the most important aspect of his work is to give people a sense of purpose, and to help them realize that they are not here by accident. Each of us comes here for specific reasons to learn specific lessons. All people, he believes, have a distant subconscious memory of their souls' eternal existence, and by helping them tap into it and find that memory and, through it, that meaning, his patients' lives are extraordinarily changed for the better.

He has discovered that souls involved in evil acts and many wrongdoings often come back as a victim of the same sort of evil in their next life. In fact, he says, what he has learned from his clients shows that beings who commit truly horrendous acts in their lifetime on earth may not return here again. They did not live well enough to deserve another human birth and a chance to redeem themselves, so their spirit dwells in regret. Sounds like an allegory for hell.

> **"After you die, you wear what you are."**
> *St. Teresa of Avi*

According to some of Newton's clients, souls returning to the between-lives space are sometimes received by a large welcoming party in the afterlife, especially after a particularly hard life. As expected, we need the comfort and assurance that close friends and family provide us. Younger souls really experience a lot of joy from this kind of huge homecoming party. When clients are met by a soul group in this way, Newton asks, "Are any of these people in your life today?" Their answers are usually, "I have been with him in many earlier lives," or "Oh, this person was my first love in high school." It's enjoyable for them to be able to see their friends and relatives as they appear in their own soul group.

An average soul group or family typically consists of around 10 to 15 souls. These are what Newton calls our "soul companions," and they are the kindred spirits that often incarnate with us as; for example, our best friend, a high-school sweetheart, a brother, or a favorite grandparent. According to Newton, parents don't often appear to us in our soul group, but they are usually nearby, within the Soul Matrix. Our primary soul mate is a soul with whom we have often been through many lifetimes. When we are given lives with this person, they are usually quite wonderful. However, a soul mate doesn't appear in every life. We have lessons to learn, and sometimes those lessons don't involve being supported by our primary soul mate, according to Newton.

Newton's clients who have had NDEs describe how the NDE, powerful enough as it is, serves only as a prelude to the actual experience of
crossing over and moving completely into the spirit world. Thus the
NDE gives us a glimpse into the initial stages of the dying experience
and provides validation as to what we will actually experience when
our physical life is over.

In Newton's experience, his subjects often think that when they reach
super-consciousness (connecting with the Soul Matrix) they will see a
well-known religious figure, such as Jesus, Mohammed, or the
Buddha. However, this is not typically what happens, which can be a
shock for those who are deeply religious. When, under hypnosis,
someone reports seeing a figure approaching them that looks to be a
religious personage, Newton will ask, "What do you see?" And he or
she will tell him, "I see my personal spiritual teacher", who turns out
not to be a particular religious figure at all. "What's interesting,"
says Newton, "and this is what really hooked me in the beginning, is
that it does not matter whether my client is deeply religious or an
atheist. Once I have them in deep hypnosis, they pretty much tell me
the same kinds of things."

Newton himself wasn't a spiritually-inclined person when he started
his practice. Beginning as an atheist and later on as an agnostic, his clients have brought him around. He now realizes that there is a higher
power at work, so that when he talks about the "superconscious" mind,
he is talking about the innermost core of our being, our immortal
selves. It is in such a state of mind that we hold these memories of our
"life between lives" and of all of the lives we have ever lived before.

> **"As far as we can discern, the sole purpose of existence
> is to kindle a light in the darkness of being."**
> *Carl Jung*

"Death is not the end, it is simply walking out of the physical form and into the spirit realm, which is our true home. It's going back home."
Stephen Christopher

Healing emotional and mental trauma is something psychologists and psychiatrists have pursued since psychotherapy began. While conventional systems of treatment do occasionally yield results, continuous innovations in methodology have the potential to be more effective. Pioneers, boldly moving into uncharted territory, are the ones that discover the breakthroughs, setting new precedents that others will follow. These innovative iconoclasts run the risk of criticism and censure from peers, but, as their therapies show consistent positive results, they eventually gain a measure of vindication.

The psycho-pharmaceutical approach, in most cases, creates only short-term alleviation of a problem. As the "default panacea" for our ills, it usually treats symptoms of a problem instead of resolving the core issue. These drugs can also have dangerous long-term physical and mental side-effects. In spite of this, neurologists and hypnotherapists have continued to delve into the mind to better understand and genuinely attempt to help heal and resolve deep-seeded issues, rooted within a patient's mind.

One treatment, known as Eye Movement Desensitization and Reprocessing (EMDR), was developed by Francine Shapiro Ph.D.. EMDR taps into REM sleep's high-speed processing mode that we all experience but have a hard time accessing consciously. Focusing on the therapist's hand, or on a wand, the patient is asked to move their eyes in a rhythmic "side to side" motion, while thinking about a specific disturbing feeling, image, or sensation. The most traumatic experiences are broken down into smaller chunks. This subsequently makes the process of dealing with traumatic events easier to assimilate and not too overwhelming.

This therapy also generates greater bilateral resonance in each hemisphere of the brain, coaxing more communication through the corpus callosum (the connective tissue bridge between the two hemispheres). A patient can overcome emotional dependency from a negative situation, helping them view a given situation dispassionately. In this way, it is an effective treatment for a wide variety of emotional issues. While hypnosis induces the patient into a relaxed and alpha/theta state of mind, EMDR increases the information processing within the brain between the hemispheres so that unresolved issues can be healed.

Allan Botkin, Ph.D. was the first doctor in the US to treat combat-related Post Traumatic Stress Disorder (PTSD) in war veterans with EMDR He has successfully treated WWII, Korean War, Vietnam War, and Desert Storm veterans, working at the VA in Chicago. Botkin found that he could routinely and quite rapidly accomplish therapeutic outcomes with EMDR to a degree that was simply not possible using traditional therapies.

In 1995, Botkin was working with a patient using EMDR and had an amazing epiphany. He accidentally discovered Induced After Death Communication (IADC) during a therapy session with a Vietnam veteran, who was disturbed by the memory and nightmares of a Vietnamese girl killed in the war. During the session, the patient had a vividly lucid vision of the dead girl face, but she look different, relaxed and happy and she let him know that everything was "okay" and that she was now at peace. This single moment of reconciliation and reassurance did more than years of traditional therapy, resolving his PTSD.

> **"This discovery has deepened my understanding of life,**
> **of people, and of my profession"**
> *Allen Botkin*

Botkin experimented with a number of variations of EMDR and made changes to the standard technique that was more effective. He tweaked the EMDR protocols, helping move patients into what he calls the "receptive mode". Using this new method, he has seen great success in treating trauma, grief, anger, guilt, sadness, and shame associated with the death of a loved one. As patients continued to report their experiences, it became clear that these IADCs were healing patients to a degree never thought possible. Grief therapists and hospice care workers continue to confirm that there are significant healings associated with spontaneous IADCs. Botkin also continues to refine his procedures, and to date IADC therapy has helped thousands of people overcome their grief and guilt, by allowing them to experience communication with the dearly departed in their lives.

"When their guilt is resolved in an IADC…
the patients conscious is actually strengthened!"
Allen Botkin

A typical IADC clinical session involves the patient vividly seeing and communicating with a deceased person and that person telling the patient that everything is "OK" and not "to grieve". In some cases, the deceased will relate previously unknown information to the patient. Later, the patient confirms, from a third party source, that the information is true.

The first time Botkin intentionally induced IADC was while working with a man who had lost his 13 year old daughter, after the child's parents had made the heart-wrenching decision to take her off life-support. After she was taken off, his daughter struggled to breathe and died in his arms. He explained how IADC was a new procedure and asked the grieving father if he wanted to give it a try. He was willing, even though he was convinced that it wouldn't work because he was an avowed atheist. After he took him through the entire procedure, he opened his eyes with a look of utter amazement and said, "I saw my daughter! She looked at me, and I could feel her love for me." He was convinced that his daughter was still alive, although in a very different place. He left the session feeling totally joyous, having reconnected with his daughter. Botkin followed up with him over a year later, and the father told him, "People don't really die. They just take on a different form and live in a different place, which is very beautiful."

A paradoxical element of IADC is that, the more skeptical a patient is, the more effective the treatment is in many cases. When Botkin explained the procedure to his patients at the VA hospital, the vast majority were very skeptical at first. However, even under these trying circumstances, his success rate was a whopping 98%! When he retired from the VA hospital and went into private practice, he began treating patients that weren't nearly as skeptical, and his success rate dropped to around 70%. He is now convinced that people who have strong beliefs about the afterlife have a more difficult time achieving ADC because their expectations interfere with the "receptive mode".

In another fascinating case, a woman had some unresolved guilt issues over a death that had occurred during her college years. A male friend of hers was undecided as to whether to come to a dance party where she was DJ-ing. She said, "I flirted a bit during a phone call, and he decided to make the drive." After he failed to arrive, she found out later that he was killed by a truck on the way there. She felt awful about the role she played in the accident, and heard about IADC. She had been expecting to meet as scruffy old psychotherapist eccentric type character. Instead, Botkin resembled a kids' Little League baseball coach.

The first thing she saw him pull out was a two-foot white stick with a blue marker cap on it, and she derisively thought, "Is this a magic wand for seeing dead people?" She thought he was pulling her leg.

During the session, he gently asked her to get in touch with any grief she had, while he began moving the wand back and forth. She was filled with images of her last interaction with her diseased friend and began to cry. After closing her eyes, her diseased friend appeared to walk out from behind a door and jumped around with youthful enthusiasm. She felt great joy at the connection but couldn't tell if she was imagining the whole thing. The friend told her she wasn't to blame herself. She also saw him playing with a little dog. They said "goodbye", and she opened her eyes...laughing at the experience.

She felt the experience was "too simple", and "too light". It was, after all, just a simple conversation with her deceased friend. Botkin mentioned how people are surprised by the light-heartedness of the IADC experience. Later, she found out that her deceased friend sister's dog had died, and it was the exact same breed and description as the one she saw in her vision! She was utterly dumbfounded. "I still don't know what's real. What I do know is that, when I think of him, I no longer dwell on the images of me calling him or of his car getting hit. Instead, I see him walking toward me, laughing and playing with a little dog. For now, this is the only kind of proof I need."

In yet another case, a daughter was stricken with grief over the loss of her father to cancer. She cried a lot, was very depressed, and wasn't responding to medications. Finally, she ended up getting referred to Botkin's clinic. She reported staying at her father's bedside for months, while a cancerous growth on his neck took his life. Botkin performed the IADC procedure, and, upon closing her eyes, she said, "He looks healthy again. He looks happy. Grandpa and grandma are with him and so are two of my aunts and an uncle. They all died some time ago. They're all partying, laughing... Oh, they're really enjoying themselves!" She opened her eyes and said she wanted to be with them right now but knew that she couldn't. Botkin started another procedure and had her hold the same thought as before. The scene came back, and her father walked up to her and said that he was still with her. He told her that she should continue to take care of her children and that he would come for her, when it was her time. She smiled with light tears streaming down her face. After leaving the office, her pain and grief over her father's death was gone. On the way out, she remarked, "That was absolutely amazing! I know that was really them."

Very few humans can kill another human being without feeling at least some degree of remorse. When a soldier kills another person, that memory of the event often becomes a blood stain on the soldier's mind. The imagery of the event reappears in numerous flashbacks throughout their lives. In many cases, the guilt over the killing becomes too great to repress, expressing itself as suffocating depression and suicide.

Many of Botkin's early patients were veterans that suffered from PTSD with effects including nightmares, depression, reoccurring flashbacks, drug addiction, and alcoholism. In one case, a veteran from the Vietnam War experienced an incident that haunted him for most of his life. There had been a long, grisly battle, and his unit was running low on ammunition. Just as all hope was fading, a helicopter arrived with much needed supplies. As he unloaded the ammunition, he looked up just in time to see an enemy soldier running towards him. Reacting quickly, he shot and killed the guy. Though it was his first time killing another human being, he felt exhilaration and in control. He didn't think much more about the incident for the remainder of his tour. After he returned home, however, he began having terrible nightmares about the incident that continued for the next twenty five years. He repeatedly saw the face of the soldier and wondered if the soldier he killed had had a family. At times, he felt great remorse and sadness. He related that, "I just feel terrible. What I did goes against everything I have ever believed."

Botkin performed the IADC procedure. Once the veteran's eyes were closed, he described what appeared to be the dead soldier's face. "It doesn't look like the soldier's face I saw in Nam and what I see in my nightmares. I see him smiling and happy." The patient sat quietly, then opened his eyes and said, "He communicated to me that he was very content where he was, and he understood that I had to do what I did." He went on to say, "I'm really surprised that the person I killed would have such feelings. This is really strange. I feel like he and I are not just 'ok' with each other; I feel like we're friends." After the session, he tried to visualize the image of the face he saw in his nightmares and found that he couldn't. A two-year follow up by Botkin revealed that the patient's nightmares of the incident had completely vanished from the day of the IADC.

Regardless of the gravity of the traumas the deceased inflicted... asking for forgiveness. In every case, the patient forgives... the anger dramatically decreases"
Allen Botkin

Some practitioners, during an IADC, seem to experience what their patients are seeing. There is a profound "simultaneous vision" of the deceased, by both the practitioner and the patient. The first time Botkin experienced this was during an IADC, as an intern sat in on one of his sessions. The intern claimed to have seen what the patient was seeing. In time, Botkin discovered there were similar occurrences with other IADC practitioners. There were cases wherein the therapist experienced spontaneous IADC with the deceased person their patient was grieving for, during sessions. During these profound experiences, the therapist received thanks for re-uniting the survivor with the deceased and to encourage the therapist to keep going on with the IACD sessions.

Nearly all of Botkin's patients are completely convinced their experiences are real, regardless of their prior belief system. Botkin has chosen not to take sides in the philosophical debate over the actual existence of an afterlife. He writes, "The IADC experience heals, and it appears that beliefs are completely inconsequential." In 2003, Botkin founded The Center for Grief and Traumatic Loss in Libertyville, Illinois. His 2006 book, *A New Therapy for Healing Grief and Trauma*, became a national best seller.

Does this validate the idea that communication with the deceased is real? Regardless, one thing is for sure. This revolutionary therapy is profoundly affecting how grief and trauma are understood and can be effectively treated. More importantly, it is a very powerful tool in helping to heal people around the world. It is clear that Botkin has accomplished significant breakthroughs in the areas of psychology, transpersonal psychology, parapsychology, metaphysics, and spirituality with this amazing therapy.

"IACD therapy should become a common tool in the psychologist's repertoire. Clinical experience based on thousands of cases at this point demonstrates that the procedure simply works. It heals patients."
Allen Botkin

Indeed, these experiences seems to convey important spiritual truths that cross all ideological beliefs, cultures, religious affiliations, ethnicities, and class distinctions. In most cases spiritually transformative events happen to people, often when they least anticipate it, and it appears there is a connection between these events, NDE, and other states of consciousness. These incidents are known to induce a heightened state of awareness and enhance human potential, leaving a memorable and life changing impact on those that experience them.

The Thread: appears there are many connections between these experiences, the nature of consciousness, and its underlying dimensional aspects. Bringing dimensionality into the equation establishes a foundation upon which we might prove the existence of soul, heaven, and our connections to it. It is the purpose of science to decode the mysteries of the unknown. It has simply evolved such that it's toolbox cannot easily quantify or prove empirically the types of perceptual experiences that can only be described not directly observed nor measured. But this book is full of persons of science and medicine who are compiling vast amounts of evidentiary data that scientific inquiry will in time peel away the layers of superstition and discover ways of measuring the immeasurable. It wasn't long ago science couldn't even measure the distance to the moon.

Classifying all the present elements into a common language for scientific reference and study, by adding new terms, is an important first step. By initiating the first steps to building and mapping a new language, we can create a periodic-type chart of qualitative metaphysical elements. Using terms that are universally understood, developed, and agreed upon by core scientific teams and theosophists will help us delve into the consistent threads that create patterns of information. Simply starting to build a lexicon with these base elements is merely a beginning. Following trends of qualified experiences, we will discover that such experiences are so consistent they are undeniable. Defining terms and synonyms of this metaphysical realm will facilitate understanding of our universal connection and the dimensional energy patterns within it, of which we are all an eternal living part.

We are all players in an infinite universal orchestra, whose collective music sings the cosmos into being. However, imagine how much more harmonious and joyous our world would be if we were to become fully conscious of our role within this divine orchestral suite, and learn to read and play from the same celestial sheet music?

As the many examples presented here show, there is a consistent thread, a clear pattern between the experiences and memories people have had from the different genres of experience we have explored. In many incidents there is verifiable data to substantiate "in fact" that individuals' supernatural experiences corroborate with those of others. Though mainstream science has yet to accept this quantum or multidimensional reality that we currently exist within, I believe the rapidly accumulation of overwhelming evidence will eventually drive a paradigm shift. This shift is underway globally, if yet by only a tiny percentage of human souls on the planet today. The 100th Monkey effect will eventually occur and drive mankind into wider perceptions and beliefs, igniting a new renaissance of the soul.

"It is not just NDErs who have to visualize on this collective level but also persons who have undergone a similar transformative experience as a result of deep spiritual awakening... it may be that NDErs and others who have had similar awakenings— collectively represent an evolutionary thrust toward higher consciousness for humanity at large"
Kenneth Ring

In the optimist's mind, this new paradigm will become common knowledge, thus making intentions transparent, helping propel humanity to a healthy understanding of itself and of ourselves individually. The greatest question is: Can we make this shift before our global house sinks into an irreversible decline?

Most people living at the pace of the modern world rarely take the opportunity to connect with their spiritual selves, other than some rare pondering. In whatever culture, religion, or metaphysical context one chooses to frame it, there exists within us an innate understanding on a deeply primordial level that we are much more than just flesh and bones, a random cosmic accident, a meaningless congregation of cellular biology.

We are conscious creatures and, unlike most animals on the planet, conscious of consciousness itself. As a result of this predicament, man finds himself in a terrifyingly thrilling position within the vast sentient continuum of life. Seemingly poised between the organic, instinctual ignorance of an animal and the blissfully free omniscience of a god, we are walking a tight rope everyday... torn between worlds both heavenly and hellish. The angels and demons of our inner nature are played out on the grand stage of life in a drama that fashions personal character and collectively, the global evolution of humanity itself.

> **"We have to recognize that we are spiritual beings with souls existing in a spiritual world as well as material beings with bodies and brains existing in a material world."**
> *Sir John C. Eccles*

Our egos mediate this internal battle between the duality of our nature, forever attempting to reconcile the mind with matter, the conscious self with the unconscious self, the spirit with the flesh, the yin and the yang. Clearly, if we are ever to untangle the twisted cords of our psychic schism, we need to learn as much as we can, so that we may live fully integrated, balanced, and spiritually-coherent lives, before we annihilate ourselves as a species.

Our current evolutionary potential remains incomplete if not regressive, but how might we begin to turn the tide? We must first start asking the right questions about our existential and inner situations before we can ever hope to forge a new paradigm of humanity.

Soul Evolution: Our souls need biological containers to grow, and as God's paintbrushes, we reflect information back to the infinite source. The source wants to see and understand itself, just like we do. It needs our DNA to continue forward, unhindered. It uses the manifestation of our genetic vibration to see and understand itself through us, as we traverse through time and space. As humans, the creation of negative or destructive situations is out of sync with our biological container (body/life), going against the natural order of our very existence in the universe. But, as an integral part of existing in the physical universe of time, all matter decays. The exponential physical expansion of our existence is hardwired into us in order to perpetuate life, not to hurt or destroy it.

> **"Peace cannot be kept by force.
> It can only be achieved by understanding."**
> *Albert Einstein*

Mankind's successful spiritual and physical evolution helps guarantee the survival of our species. But this also ensures at a dimensional level that souls have a place to manifest themselves, to reside, explore, and grow. Souls are continually bringing truth and universal information back to the source "God", like honey bees bringing pollen back to the hive. Each soul is on what Joseph Campbell identified as 'the hero's journey', confronting challenges, defeating inner monsters, learning from hard experience, and returning to the heavenly village with stories that enlighten and contribute to the universal experience of evolving.

The healthy and prosperous continuity of our existence helps the spiritual growth of the heavenly community that is the Soul Matrix, within the infinite source of love. It allows "God" to see, understand, and experience "itself" through us. The infinite love source needs us and we need it—it's a symbiotic relationship. We are the cells within the body of god, we are all collectively one. We do not exist without it. Everything is made from its fabric, wrapping around our world and all things like a baby in the womb. This occurs at another dimensional level, adding love and positivity around all of us to help assure our next steps in this physical journey—a journey we all willfully chose at a deeper subconscious level, to arrive here especially now during these changing and challenging times on earth. The age of complacency is ending; a new perspective is awakening within us. The time is now. Higher consciousness evolution is in the works at a planetary level, and we are nearing a critical mass for transformational change.

> **"Where ignorance is our master, there is no possibility of real peace."**
> *Dalai Lama XIV*

Synergistic Order: The spiritual universe has a synergistic order, of which some individuals have gotten a glimpse. We cannot continue to accept negative social, religious, scientific, and medical pressure telling us what is unnatural and unreal. This negative belief is archaic and ignorant, and unacceptable. Doctors persistently tell people point blank, "You shouldn't talk about this" after a person has had the most powerful experience of their life. This antiquated belief is old-world thinking. There is now data that these experiences are very likely to be real—we are connected to an eternal and infinite source of love that governs the universe, which we currently know very little about.

> **"Rationalism and doctrinairism are the diseases of our time... Our concept of space and time only approximate validity..."**
>
> *Carl Jung*

This order does not fall under any specific group's religious, ethnic, historical, or personal title. Iconic structures, contrived to inherently spread truth, but a power so great is hard to handle. Humanity's spiritual ignorance has led many individuals into corruption, inadvertently and naively throughout history. Such manipulation and destruction is humanity's downfall, and it is largely due to the *words* that are used. Thoughts follow words which become perception, or belief; words interject ideas, and the manifestation of those ideas. Words have to be transparent so they match the thoughts and intentions behind them. Without this transparency, there can be no corresponding pictures and the vision is lost, wreaking havoc in its wake. The words of the expanded spiritual language taken from those that have traversed to the other side inherently tend to be pure and clean and clear of negativism, distrust, violence, hate and most of the other ills of human suffering. The other side is from where we come and where we go, who else better to know, than people who have been there?

We enter the ocean of life, knowing this wave will carry us on a ride—one we will do our best to aim for—which determines where we will end up. Deep inside of human consciousness, we carry the collective archetypal image, a blueprint of physical survival based on spiritual values, because it is what truly drives us at our deepest core level.

Our species' evolution is dependent on sound and rational productive steps to guarantee its existence in the physical universe. This instinct resides within us all as part of our DNA. It is now time to bring our intuitive center to the surface level our individual awareness, to allow it to help guide us.

> " All our lives and inter-lives lie within that infinity, as do the karmic patterns which shape personal evolutionary development… Most importantly, knowledge of the inter-life intensified personal responsibility… Earth being no more than a very necessary testing ground conductive to spiritual evolution."
>
> *Joe Fisher*

A Challenge to Achieve: For civilization to thrive, we need to recondition ourselves to the belief that the spiritual world is as real than the physical world. If a four thousand person meditation has the ability to reduce crime in a major city by 25%, just think what millions or billions can do with this type of collective power (*Power of the Collective,* Hegelin, 1993). Through collective, positive intention, we have the potential to creatively affect change.

Emotion creates peptide chemical changes in our brain. This cascade of effects fuels and runs the neural network within our brains, which may have the ability to connect us with our higher dimensional self – our source.

If inter-dimensional communication is connected to our neural network within the brain, optogenetics technology might offer a means to target specific neurons activating bio-chemical receptors to enhance a state of hyper-dimensional consciousness. The techniques mentioned in this book can enhance our ability to see through the veil into the other side, allowing us to see ourselves as the eternal beings we are. Crossing this threshold allows us to see situations from a greater perspective, with higher dimensional guidance, enabling humans to make lucid and sensible decisions especially important when world leaders are making life-changing decisions every day that affect us.

This type of consciousness understanding technology is in its infancy stage, I believe its future holds much promise. These trans-dimensional therapies given the proper attention, funding, university support could become one of the important scientific breakthroughs in human history. The social implications of human introspection at such a level could only help lead mankind to align with its higher ethical self.

It would seem plausible if in the case pre-youth individuals were able to view a more in-depth understanding or see themselves (and the world) from a higher-dimensional state, it could give them a wider perspective of life itself. Possibility helping them remember that altruistic state of existence that we are all from, and eternally a part of. Seeing this prior to their brains fully maturing, but old enough to understand the human condition would be an optimal point. Seeing within their deeper self, could and would inspire individuals to act with social conscience, knowing that all things are connected together and every forward gesture, movement and action through "Time" does make a difference.

Could these new transcendental therapies as described herein be the catalyst for human growth? If a generation of people could see deeply within themselves could it become the catalyst needed to resolve our current earthy condition?

Evolutionary quantum leaps occur when a species is faced with extinction. Now, [we are] at such a threshold...
Alberto Volloldo

Many scientific publications have released articles and research data pointing out how scientists now definitively support the theory that other unseen dimensions exist and occupy the same space as us. This mainstream scientific theory is only recently beginning to be understood as evidence supporting this concept, and it continues to grow.

At the biological level, scientific researchers are able to measure and document changes in chemicals receptors, brain waves, neuron activity, biophotonic discharge and human magnetic/electric fields. Doing these measurements during different states of consciousness might increase our understanding and potentially explain or support what today is mere conjecture. What might be learned should we measure biological, chemical or neurological activity at moments before and after death, during intercourse, conception, playing music, singing, massage, exercise, yoga, chanting and other Trans-Dimensional Experiences such as:

141

- Hypnotic Regression
- Induced After Death Communication (IADC)
- Dream States (Lucid & Nightmare)
- Meditation (Transcendental)
- Out-of-Body Experience (OBE)
- Human Energy Field Manipulation (psychokinesis)
- Extra Sensory Perception
- Meditation
- Prayer and Projected Intention
- Remote Viewing
- Post-Mortem Communication
- Shared Death Experience
- Auditory Stimulation (hemisphere sound pulse manipulation)
- EMDR (rapid eye movement desensitization & reprocessing)
- Temporal Lobe and electrode-stimulation
- Sensory Deprivation Chambers/Floatation Tanks
- Medium & Channeling States
- Chemically Induced Altered States
- Shamanism / Tantric States
- Song: om, chant, affirmation, harmonizing, singing, drumming & playing music
- Holotropic breath-work, trance/meditative rhythm breathing

Possibilities also include the use of an optogenetic analysis and stimulation equipment, like a Stimoceiver from the 1960's, an electroencephalogram for analyzing brain waves, or with the use of a photomultiplier to record data about photo-biological energy fields.

Advanced technology has many new options for measurement and analysis. All these activities, therapies, and situations affect the human state and the measurable biochemical energetic response. The human eye may not see energy, but energy is quantifiable there.

When the soul is gone those measurable elements also vanish. I am optimistic that technology has the potential to quantify data in this new scientific frontier. Ultimately making this parallel dimension measurable will take the assembling and unification of leading researchers. Parapsychologists, neurologists, scientists, quantum physicists and phenomenological experts are merely beginning to study the spiritual aspects of our existence. That is a good thing but only a start.

Unifying scientific, religious, and spiritual organizations with a common language of the spirit when researching a better understanding of the soul and its connection to the source is a wise course of action. It is time to develop the alphabet of a new spiritual language—the continuity of our existence might depend on it. I feel redefining concepts and terms for use in a scientific, spiritual, and therapeutic communities to create a standardized platform is important. With intention set on harmonizing humanity with a communication language congruent with our higher dimensional thoughts.

Human DNA demands individual and species survival. It may be that it's inherent in our DNA to evolve and develop this spiritual consciousness for the survival of humanity so that the souls (the unseen and unconscious part of our physical being) have a place to grow, learn and evolve.

The more we continue to ask questions, the more the answers will unfold. Humanity's evolutionary destiny is to forge a pathway for continual growth, knowledge, and a more complete understanding of who we really are, and "what's really going on".

"Ye shall know the truth and the truth shall set you free"
John 8:32

We all come here with the awareness that there will be difficult experiences to overcome and that we must continuously push forward to achieve our goals. If we accept the reports of those who have, through NDE's or any of the other trans-dimensional experiences discussed in this book, traversed to the other side, our spirit's intention of remembering the place of love from which we came, and to spread and teach unconditional love as our soul's highest purpose, may manifest in our reality.

Understanding inner truth has the potential to move us to a higher operating level, past the physical shell, beyond the thinking mind, and deep within the soul, where we can clearly identify and connect with our eternal source.

"Every human being should realize that the future of humanity is dependent on their present actions and thinking."

Dalai Lama XIV

ACKNOWLEDGEMENTS

I want to personally thank all the people that took their time to be interviewed for this project, and the individuals that had written books, journals, and articles on these topics and for their inspiring contributions to the research and understanding of the soul's journey. Thanks to Kirsten Miller for access to the Berkeley Psychic Institute publishing department library. Thanks to Michelle Nassopoulos for giving me a monthly column and then her having to painstakingly edit my articles for *Psychic Reader* magazine.

Thanks to the International Association of Near Death Studies for providing interview privileges with speakers and attendees; that was a tremendous experience and a major help for this book.

Another key building block for attaining and assembling this information was my personal friend Manuel Inverno. His assistance and resources enabled me to secure travel and attend events in order to obtain interviews and data in developing this book. He also had many lucid and creative concepts helping me to form some of the early ideas that eventually became this book.

My spiritual mentor Edward Salisbury who has inspired me on this path of knowledge and growth. His encouragement and motivation not only helped with the progression of this book, it also ended up including the resurrection of the Central Texas IANDS chapter, which has been an enlightening and educating experience.

Dan Terry and Shane Matthews for their editing and development input on the book, adding literary contributions, formatting, organizing and creating its cohesiveness. To friend, author Michael Somers for his inspiration and support and allowing me to feel as a creative mind for him to consult during his writing process. His book *Galactic Exodus: Counterdance of the Cybergods* is of epic proportions.

Of course, my son Luca, whose existence on this terrestrial physical plane has added and inspired me to new heights of compassion and understanding. His own very early in-depth memories and personal experiences has inspired the completion of this project as a travel guide for him and others of future generations to understand metaphysical and spiritual information without confusing narratives, conditions or dogma.

SPECIAL APPRECIATION

An extra big thanks to my Mom, Patricia DeBow and my Dad, Raleigh DeBow for being supportive parents and for all of the love and opportunities I received, I truly appreciate it.

PERSONAL INSPIRATION

Mother, Father, Siblings, Grandparents, immediate and extended family, Michael Somers, Sandra DeBow, Brian Hulbert, Michelle Nassopoulos, Michael Shuster, Kirstin Miller, Jon Stark, Edward Salisbury, Nancy Noret Moore, Alex Forbes, Dana Hodgson, Cheryl Mackin, Mike Cummins, Jesse Villagran, Dan Terry, Bill Levinson, Brian & Brenda Leonard, Manuel Inverno, Freddy Tista, John Strisower, Greig Broussard, David Olszewski, Theodore Charles Oliphant III, Gayla Reider, David Cuddy, James Chankin, William Aguiar, Nathan Bryan, Pat & Jodi Johnson, Paul Davids, Victor Moore, Marianne Heer, Terrie Carr, Kristine Todd, Kerry Burkland, Dave Dean, Angela Lloyd, Thad Garbarino, Mark Callahan, Ariel Green, John Holroyt, Kurt Wedgly, Arne Haugland, Bryan Jordan, Vincent DePass, Gary Wimmer, Bill Swail, Vlad Coot, Sheri Gardener, Alfonzo Amey, Thomas Underwood, Danny Montinagro, Diego Erausquin, Michael Ames, Bob Chainey, Tom Linthicum, Sheri Oberstein, Terry Parsons, Art Takeshita, Hurly Young, Gary Binas, Melina Collazo, Gabrielle Chavez, Jemma Mulholland, Gene Liptson, Toni Bennett, Lynn Foster, James Arthur, Monica Smith, Charley Dunfield, Ian Christopher, Fred Bell, Mary Cummins, Brian Hall, Harlan Dietrich, Kevin Johnson, Patrick Flanagan, Trey Sherman, Victoria Jack, Dave Korman, Phyllis Parsons, John Alderton, Tom Davies, Scott Steers, Michael Tsarion, Bob Speilman, Greg Somers, Keith Pearson, Al Smith, Henry Sullivan, Stefan Phillips, Steven Vercher, Barbara Vaughan, Brian Walls, Micheal Tsarian, Dale Frost, Aaron Astorga, John Klimo, Nathan Wyss, Judy McBride, Warren Smith, Corina Trujillo, Fox DuQue, Corina Trujillo, John McConnell, Ken Pouge, Karena Mahoney, Peter Brothers, Mandy Begley, Ian Christopher, Ryan Wood, Kurt Johnson, Collette Middleton, Tim Clark, John Barney, Kevin Bernie, John

Kockos, Gene Lipsom, Robert Mitchell, Mike Gahon, Orville Smith, Pete Brothers, Keith Peterson, Len Saputo, Kirt Macroft, Annabelle Chan, Edward Wagner, Dan Brannon, Eugene Barnett, Andy Limbaugh, Brian Whaley, Any Starky, Zack Ward, Brook Luciano, JR Reynolds, Hurley Young, Todd Forman, Avril Calderon, Seth Ashby, Didi Seddick, Michael Lites, Brian Montone, Mark Afshire, Ted Edwards, Kent Gordon, Kimchi Moyer, Lisa Kolstad, Mark Hoffman, Allen Tatomer, Vicky Yea, Tiffany Ingram, Tara Wood, Shaun Shoemake, Shantel Mackey, Eduardo Longoria, Patricia Mandell, Rudy Rudinski, Ray Wharton, Mark Commerford, Iris Martinez, Madai Dimas, John Jacobs, Mark Devito, Rick Guerrero, Nysa Lane, Curtis Laipple, Robert Brownstein, Michael Abedin, Leslie Bailey, Shawn Schreiber, Jon Boren, Georgia Brauer, Deanna Brochin, Roger Chan, Kevin Crique, Jim Dever, Jim Delettoso, Christopher Durst, Christopher Fox, Gerry Gunnick, John Harris, Ernie Hatton, Barbara Holden, Justin Kenyon, Helena Lathinen, Gracie Cassnova, CJ MacDonald, Tabatha Gibbons, Brandon Shortly, Mark Lane, Rebecka Marcias, John Hubbs, Brian Gill, John Gates, Christopher Cogswell, Mike Lorenz, Carlos Hughes, Mike Matel, Jeff Turk, Jay McMillan, Glenn Marcell, Billy Hardy, MK Chiu, Noland Apostle, Mark Krenek, Alisha Hill, Scott Burleson, Mike Van Dyke, Phil Van Galen, Scott Johnson, Steve Friend, Darrel Belvins, Sheri Kelly, Gary Bentwolly, Robert Fraga, Dean Withers, Jonathan Saenz, Christina Green, Steve Poff, Jason St. Jillian, Ron Ugale, Kevin Cecotto, Ricky Gates, Kevin Wylie, Sean Freeze, Brett Berkette, Craig Stokes, Bart Davis, Ian Place, Shawn El Sasser, Anita & Mike Scott, Phyllis Gasper, Roxanne Massey, Mac McGruder, Robert Michell, George Humphrey, Harold Montgomery, Whitney Gilky, Arttemus Keszainn, Steve Montignani, Boris Zemelman, Darrell Brager, MJ Paul, Devon Perry, James Pickett, RD Wright, Mark Yawn, NAlmeida, Tom Schnorr, Tim Westergren, Julianne Skeetoe, Judy Coop, Kathleen Fairchild, Terri Brown, Bob Brown and family, The Sabino, Cummins, Farmer, Bensinger, Jensen, Goldeen, Barney, Bonnell, Clark, Garbarino, Ames, Gruber, Makall, Chaney, Jones, Callahan, Levinson, Rogers, Blume, Cassani, Houston, Raywanda and Inverno families. Tsugswa Brothers, Susan Hull Bostwick & Berkeley Psychic Institute team, Travis, Dalton, Mike, Sason, Marcos, Kyle, Lori, Jamaican Mark, Louie, Dusty, Joey, Yasic, Derk, Red, Daniela, Dina, Wanda, Raven, Diva, Faith, Coco, Lobo, Marcel, Big B, Jonny G, Fred Freddy, Jackhammer, Rip,

Maclom, Garbarator, Gummins, Dan'l, Mr K, Lucanator, Maximus, Funguy, Shrougy, Bongo Man, JG, Jonny Jr, BB, Bic, Thrustin, Timmyology, JCob, Petard, Nobbert, Scammy, JP, K2, Turly, Scout, Trinidady, Papa Via, Spuky, Barnegon, Gummy Seamers, Gronk, Affy, McBunge, Mr. Ballistic, Shag, Mad Dog, Big Ray, Pumper, Gum Roach, Boulder, Turly, Husky, Wiggy, Junior, Peturbo, Danage, Bich, Nutball, Squarehead, Snott Horras, Rush and Crappens.

APPENDIX A
International Association for Near Death Studies (IANDS)

The *International Association for Near-Death Studies* was founded in 1978. It is the only membership organization in the world devoted to providing information about near-death and related experiences. IANDS was created by John Audette, Kenneth Ring, Raymond Moody, and Bruce Grayson. Their mission is to provide support for NDErs, investigate the phenomenon, and disseminate their findings to experiencers, researchers, educators, heath care providers, and the general public. The organization supports research, publishes information and they also aid people in the grieving process. IANDS encourages the formation of community discussion and support groups.

The quarterly journal, *Vital Signs*, includes professional and statistical studies, accounts of NDEs, events, and related news. There are chapters around the world that provide support to experiencers, hold meetings, and facilitate speaker events. IANDS maintains a website at www.IANDS.com, which is an excellent resource of information for people to get feedback on their NDE. They also hold annual conferences in different cities around the country, and publish webinars and host videos on youtube.com for public viewing. A typical conference consists of authors, speakers, experiencers, and a series of various research studies.

One of IANDS' missions is to get this kind of information into hospitals, medical literature, and medical schools. Currently, IANDS has approximately 1,000 members internationally, with tens of thousands that have attended their meetings and conferences. Their board of directors consists of medical doctors, psychiatrists, psychologists, and other professionals. They have no religious affiliations, nor are they affiliated with any other groups. IANDS remains impartial and open-minded to the presentation of the NDE from varying points of view. Another thing IANDS helps with is spousal support programs.

IANDS is a non-profit organization focused on education and support for near-death experiences. Annual memberships are offered and donations are welcome.

International Association of Near Death Studies2741 Campus Walk Avenue, Building 500Durham, NC 27705-8878919-383-7940 IANDS.org   membership@iands.org Donate - http://iands.org/about-iands/tax-deductible.html

APPENDIX B
"Compassion in Action" The Twilight Brigade

Dannion Brinkley is one of the few individuals portrayed in a full-length network NDE docudrama while still alive. But he has died, not just once, on several occasions, and come back to tell us about it. It seems these events caused him to have an enlightened standpoint, and maybe now he sees life from a higher dimensional perspective. No matter what, these experiences have left an indelible imprint on his consciousness. Does Brinkley now have a deeper understanding of important values and key issues human kind needs to address and embrace? He has clearly pointed out some social behaviors we all have to face and improve upon if we are to become an active part of positive change.

His vision has created an accredited and award winning organization. The fact is that too many people are dying alone, and we need to stop ignoring this unrecognized minority. Every day thousands of people are dying alone. In many cases people in their end times can end up warehoused within an uncaring medical system. Brinkley's mission since 1977 has been to raise awareness about dying to ensure no one dies alone. According to the U.S. Census as of 2013, if only half died alone, it would still amount to over 3,000 people a day. He points out how archaic, haphazard, and fear based our current care is for the dying, and says "We have much more to do to improve their last days." His objective is to promote volunteering, recruitment, and education. Plus, we must integrate this palliative system into healthcare on a wider scale. As former military, Brinkley has a natural affinity to veterans, and his father was a veteran. Where he got his own experience was taking his veteran (World War II) dad in for care. He feels veterans are under appreciated for their service and valor to the United States, and he testified before congress about end of life issues for veterans and all people. A quote from Dannion.com: "The hardest thing is being alone on this bed. When a Twilight Brigade came to see me I felt appreciated and proud. Thank you my dear friends. Thank you so very much." — *Lt. Walter Foreman, Airman.*

Brinkley's organization has mobilized thousands of volunteers currently providing this new and improved complementary palliative end of life care. His team works in Veterans Administration hospitals, nursing homes and assisted living facilities throughout the United States. To date, his organization has trained over 5,000 individuals, but in a country of 300 million this number needs to multiply. Some individuals come to training to learn about end of life issues and new ways to address end of days care, care for a love one or simply for their own piece of mind. His innovative system in some cases might include: music therapy, acupuncture, guided imagery or therapeutic touch, among other things to make a person's end of life more enjoyable and less fearful. The training is a 20 hour intensive that follows national hospice and medical guidelines. The Twilight Brigade is a 501c 3 non-profit organization and operates on donations and nominal training fees. Remember at tax time , any support can be written off. Sponsor a friend or stranger in need.

"Powerful, dynamic and life changing." Are some of the words used to describe the training. This is a modified version of bullets summarizing The Twilight Brigade training:

- How to provide unconditional positive regard
- Attendee resolves own fears about death
- Develop new vocabulary of communication skills
- Help others with death fears
- Being able to recognize emotional and spiritual issues
- Shown how to be fully present with client
- How to facilitate life review with emphasis on appreciation & closure
- Understand the principles of pain management
- Learn how to interface with family member dynamic
- Develop respect for differences in spiritual, cultural, social, personal beliefs
- Understand differences without imposing own belief or value
- How to sincerely listen, while refraining from problem solving
- Become familiar with hospice philosophy
- Importance of timely referrals to social workers, psychologist, chaplain, etc.
- What to do, and how to be with the dying
- Understanding the grieving process
- Addressing personal fears and unresolved issues, things holding back from service

- Developing self-care techniques to avoid becoming burnt-out of being of service
- Team interface, utilizing resources and support
- How to maintain privacy and confidentially

In completing the course you will receive professionally and nationally recognized certificate once completed. Refer to TheTwilightBrigade.com for the PDF training session course description.

Many of those bullet points look as if they would be helpful for anybody to understand. All of us have dealt or will deal with these situations in our lives. Knowing how to navigate with some kind of advanced or professional knowledge about the issues at hand would obviously be helpful.

The Twilight Brigade is not hospice, but those values are fully embraced. Its focus is;

- Education
- Advocacy
- Service

The training focus is to develop communication skills, proper procedures when accepting assignments, correct procedures at death and always being sensitive to culture/ belief to avoid inadvertently offending clients.

The organization has been recognized by the Joint Commission on Accreditation of Healthcare Organizations and was picked by the Veterans Administration to help create a standardized model for end-of-life care. He pointed out "I am extremely proud of the fact we have the best volunteer caregivers training… and trainers in the country."

The Twilight Brigade was featured and published as a favorite charity in "Oprah Magazine". He also won the highest honor award from the National Hospice and Palliative Care Association, attended meetings with the National Academy of Sciences, and numerous Alternative Medicine Advisory Committees. Brinkley's persistence has resulted in him becoming a pioneer and leader in this field. The Twilight Brigade in now in several cities and growing.

Sadly, veterans and people around the world are dying everyday alone. Dying should not be a place of fear and loneliness. The positive retrospective values of Brinkley's organization - recognize that a life lived, the next phase in our eternal journey, and connecting with the elderly can be a treasure of knowledge, history, and insight. I have personally talked with several people who have volunteered for Brinkley's organization and they say it is an enlightening experience.

I think what they are teaching is not only a new language for the dying, but an important form of communication in everyday life, fundamentally being in a good state of mind, neutral to our own thoughts and beliefs. As if looking down at situations from a heightened perspective, not allowing conditioned beliefs, social frameworks, and cultural ideas impact communication. I consider this Brigade training as an powerful tool that humanity should learn, and an important course for a new spiritual language.

The Twilight Brigade
P.O. Box 84013   Los Angeles, California 90073
11301 Wilshire Blvd. Bldg. 258, Room 113,
Los Angeles, CA 90073
310-473-1941
310-473-1951 Fax
TheTwilightBrigade.org
admin@thetwilightbrigade.org
Donate - http://www.thetwilightbrigade.com/contact.htm

Trans-Dimensional Therapy

Allan Botkin is training licensed therapists who have completed the first weekend of EMDR training. One day training is provided on an individual basis. If interested therapists would like to include eligible colleagues and coordinate the trip, group rates are offered. Botkin is available to do IADC® training on either a Saturday or Sunday. The training day begins at 9 am and ends at 4 pm. If you are flying in from out of state, you will likely want to stay at the Hampton Inn & Suites which is right next to Botkin's office and about 30 minutes from O'Hare airport. Their address is 1400 N. Milwaukee Ave., Lincolnshire IL, 60069, and their phone number is 847-478-1400. It is suggested you fly in the day before your training, and fly out in the early evening on your training day.

Training Details; You must bring a copy of some proof that you completed the first weekend of EMDR training. The morning and early afternoon sessions consist of the basic changes to standard EMDR and a detailed description of the IADC® procedure. Also covered are screening, measurement, and contract issues. If you chose to experience the IADC® procedure yourself, it is advised that you do your training on a Saturday, and remain available for a follow-up session on Sunday morning, in the event that an additional session is necessary.

Certified IADC® trainers:
Graham Maxey, Arlington, Texas
Juliane Grodhues, Saarbrucken, Germany
Cesar Valdez, Ann Arbor, Michigan
Gary Beaver, Twin Cities, Minnesota

IADC® Training
Center for Grief and Traumatic Loss, LLC
250 Parkway Drive, Suite 150,
Lincolnshire, IL 60069
Allan L. Botkin, Psy.D.   **Email: DrAL53@aol.com**
847-680-0279   •   **Induced-ADC.com**

The RavenHeart Center Training Institute (RHCTI)

RHCTI offers programs both for those who wish to become a professional regression therapist and for anyone who desires to deepen their own spiritual journey and impact the New Humanity. This unique program is designed to prepare individuals who wish to learn to conduct PLR and who may desire to learn to gain skills in Life Between Lives Spiritual Regression.

Participants who simply wish to deepen and inform their own soul's journey, but may not wish to use this skill in a private practice, are also welcome. Our training program focuses on the technique to guide clients into sufficient trance depth to access both Past Life and entry into the Spiritual Realm. Various regression tools and techniques necessary to prepare the client for a Theta level trance experience will be taught during this training. The added dimension of crossing into Spirit requires additional skill to move a client smoothly and with care through a significant past life to the death scene, exiting the body and transitioning through the spiritual realm gateway. Prerequisites: Basic understanding of hypnosis and the hypnotic trance induction process.

The RavenHeart Center Training Institute (RHCTI)
3140 Stevens Circle S.
Erie, CO 80516
303-818-0575
Earl & Linda Backman
RavenHeartCenter.com
Linda@RavenheartCenter.com
Earl@RavenheartCenter.com

The Michael Newton Institute

If you feel drawn towards becoming a Life Between Lives Hypno-therapy practitioner you are almost certainly listening and responding to your soul's calling – and its own quest for growth. Become a quali-fied and experienced hypnotherapy practitioner. Once you have com-pleted hypnotherapy training and are qualified in hypnotherapy and have the required clinical hypnosis experience with clients you should focus on training and gaining experience in past life regres-sion regression techniques.

Past Life Regression Training options are available through the Alli-ance Training Program. Locate TNI's scheduled LBL training events for each year, and formally apply to register for one of our training courses. Once accepted you can progress to working towards certific-ation with TNI as a Life Between Lives practitioner, facilitating cli-ents' journeys to the inter-life in order to awaken an understanding of their immortal identity. It is a fulfilling, rewarding and humbling ex-perience to facilitate such sessions and as LBL practitioners, it is a sacred and fulfilling offer of service to our clients as they learn, dis-cover and remember fascinating aspects of their soul lineage. All ap-plications must be supported by documentation such as copies of rel-evant certificates of qualification. Only qualified and experienced hypnosis practitioners will be accepted for TNI Life Between Lives training. Full details of requirements will be supplied on your regis-tration form. TNI Life Between Lives trainings are training courses developed, authorized and sanctioned by Michael Newton, the Founder The Newton Method of LBL hypnotherapy.

The Michael Newton Institute for Life Between Lives
Hypnotherapy
1121 Military Cutoff Road, Suite C312
Wilmington, North Carolina
NewtonInstitute.org

Institute of Noetic Sciences (IONS)

Broadening our knowledge of the nature and potentials of mind and consciousness and applying that knowledge to enhancing human well-being and the quality of life on the planet is the Institute of Noetic Sciences mission.

The Institute of Noetic Sciences serves an emerging movement of globally conscious citizens dedicated to manifesting our highest capacities. We believe that consciousness is essential to a paradigm shift that will lead to a more sustainable world. We encourage open-minded explorations of consciousness through the meeting of science and spirit. We take inspiration from the great discoveries of human history that have been sourced from insight and intuition and that have harnessed reason and logic for their outer expression. It is our conviction that systematic inquiries into consciousness will catalyze positive concrete transformations in the world. In this process, our vision is to help birth a new worldview that recognizes our basic interconnectedness and interdependence and promotes the flourishing of life in all its magnificent forms.

Institute of Noetic Sciences (IONS)
625 2nd St., Suite 200
Petaluma, CA 94952-5120
707-775-3500
707-781-7401
info@noetic.org

The Monroe Institute

The Monroe Institute furthers the exploration of consciousness, expanded awareness and discovery of self through technology, education, research and development. It provides experiential education programs facilitating the personal exploration of human consciousness. The Institute also serves as the core of a research affiliation investigating the evolution of human consciousness and making related information available to the public. The Institute is devoted to the premise that focused consciousness contains solutions to the major issues of human experience.

The Institute propose is to introduce or enhance abilities that will constructively change humankind's direction and destiny.We are a nonprofit charitable organization furthering the evolution of human consciousness through our educational programs and associated research. The Institute is internationally known for its participatory educational programs that provide opportunities for the personal exploration of expanded states of consciousness.

The Monroe Institute
365 Roberts Mountain Road
Faber, Virginia 22938
Toll Free 866-881-3440
434-361-1500
info@monroeinstitute.org
TheMonroeInstitute (skype)

The Weiss Institute
PO Box 560788
Miami, Florida 33256-0788
fax: 305-598-4009

OPUS Organization For Paranormal Understanding and Support
Lester Valez
408-268-2837
Facebook: OPUS

Model of Associated Human Experiences that induce Cosmic or Spiritual Awakenings

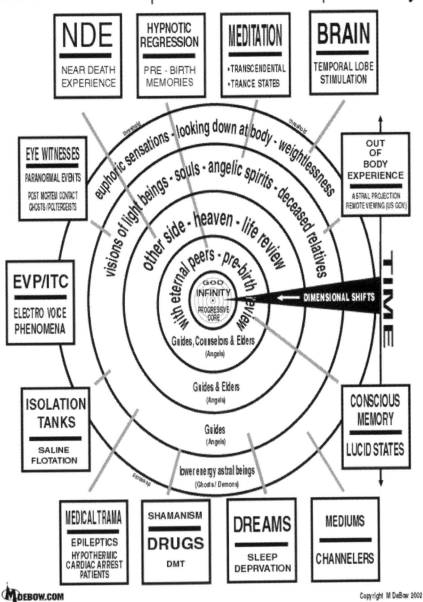

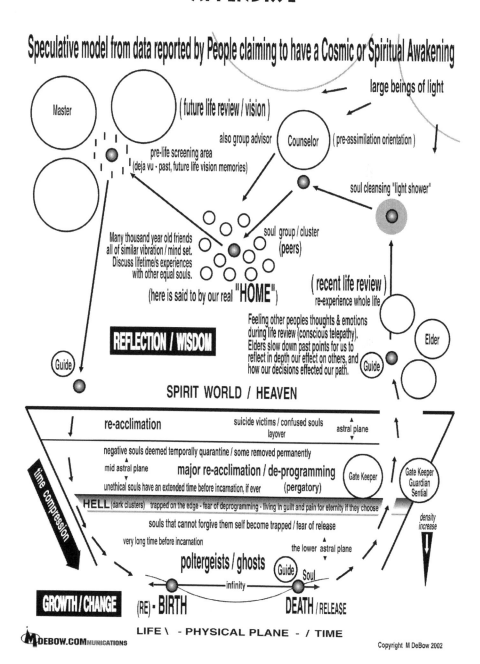

Speculative model from data reported by People claiming to have a Cosmic or Spiritual Awakening

large beings of light

Master

(future life review / vision)

also group advisor   Counselor   (pre-assimilation orientation)

pre-life screening area
(deja vu - past, future life vision memories)

soul cleansing "light shower"

soul group / cluster
(peers)

Many thousand year old friends
all of similar vibration / mind set.
Discuss lifetime/s experiences
with other equal souls.

(recent life review)
re-experience whole life

(here is said to by our real "HOME")

REFLECTION / WISDOM

Feeling other peoples thoughts & emotions
during life review (conscious telepathy).
Elders slow down past points for us to
reflect in depth our effect on others, and
how our decisions effected our path.

Elder

Guide   Guide

SPIRIT WORLD / HEAVEN

re-acclimation   suicide victims / confused souls   astral plane
                                          layover

negative souls deemed temporally quarantine / some removed permanently

mid astral plane   major re-acclimation / de-programming   Gate Keeper

unethical souls have an extended time before incarnation, if ever   (pergatory)

Gate Keeper
Guardian
Sential

time compression

HELL (dark clusters)   trapped on the edge - fear of deprogramming - living in guilt and pain for eternity if they choose

souls that cannot forgive them self become trapped / fear of release

density
increase

very long time before incarnation   the lower astral plane

poltergeists / ghosts   Guide Soul

infinity

GROWTH/CHANGE   (RE) - BIRTH   DEATH / RELEASE

LIFE \ - PHYSICAL PLANE - / TIME

APPENDIX F

INTERPRETIVE MODEL

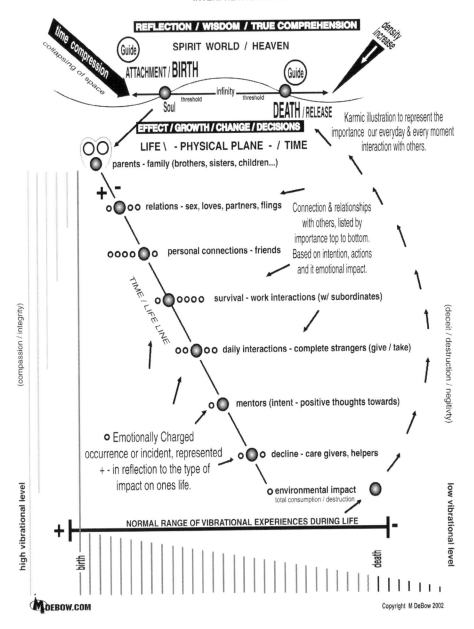

REFLECTION / WISDOM / TRUE COMPREHENSION

time compression

collapsing of space

density increase

(Guide) SPIRIT WORLD / HEAVEN

ATTACHMENT / **BIRTH**

(Guide)

infinity

threshold   threshold

Soul

DEATH / RELEASE

Karmic illustration to represent the importance our everyday & every moment interaction with others.

EFFECT / GROWTH / CHANGE / DECISIONS

LIFE \ - PHYSICAL PLANE - / TIME

parents - family (brothers, sisters, children...)

+ -

relations - sex, loves, partners, flings

Connection & relationships with others, listed by importance top to bottom. Based on intention, actions and it emotional impact.

personal connections - friends

TIME / LIFE LINE

survival - work interactions (w/ subordinates)

daily interactions - complete strangers (give / take)

mentors (intent - positive thoughts towards)

o Emotionally Charged occurrence or incident, represented + - in reflection to the type of impact on ones life.

decline - care givers, helpers

environmental impact
total consumption / destruction

(compassion / integrity)

(deceit / destruction / negitivity)

high vibrational level

low vibrational level

+ NORMAL RANGE OF VIBRATIONAL EXPERIENCES DURING LIFE -

birth

death

162

BIBLIOGRAPHY

Atwater, P. M. H., Lh.D. *Beyond The Light* Avon 2009

Atwater, P. M. H., Lh.D. *Coming Back To Life* Ballantine Books 2008

Atwater, P.M.H., Lh. D. *Children of the New Millennium*, Three Rivers Press 1999

Alexander, Eben, M.D. *Proof of Heaven* Simon & Shuster 2012

Backman, Linda, www.RavenHeartCenter.com 2014 2014

Bedi, Ashok, M.D. *Path to the Soul* Weiser Books 2000

Bodkin, Allan, L. Psy.D., Hogan, Craig, R. PhD. *Induced After Death Communication* Hampton Rhodes, 1999

Brinkley, Dannion Personal Interview, San Francisco, CA, 2001

Brinkley, Dannion, Perry, Paul *Saved by the Light* Harper 1995

Brinkley, Dannion, Perry, Paul *At Peace in the Light* Harper 1996

Brinton, W. Personal Interview, Seattle, WA, 2001

Brumbly, M.D. Personal Interview, Seattle, WA, 2001

Carman, Neil & Elizabeth, Personal Interview Seattle, WA, 2001, Austin, TX 2013

Carman , Neil & Elizabeth, *Cosmic Cradle* North Atlantic Books 2000, 2013

DeBow, Matt, *LIGHT: Health Benefits & Medical Applications*, 2012, Austin, TX

Doore, Gary, Ph. D., Editor, *What Survives?* Tarcher Inc.1990

Eadie, Betty Personal Interview, Seattle, WA 2001

Eadie, Betty, Curtis A. Taylor, *Embraced By The Light* Bantam 1992

Faulkner, Raymond O., Translator *Ancient Egyptian Book of the Dead* 1972

Fenimore, Angie, *Beyond The Darkness* Bantam 1995

Fox, Mark, *Religion, Spirituality and the NDE* Routledge 2003

Forie, Edith, Ph.D. *Have You Been Here Before* Ballantine Books 1978

Forie, Edith, Ph.D. *Unquiet Dead* Ballantine Books 1987

Fisher, Joe, *The Case For Reincarnation* Bantam 1985

Gerlich et al, *Nature Communications* 2:263, 2011

Greyson, Bruce, M.D. Personal Interview, Seattle, WA 2001

Grant, Robert, J. *The Place We Call Home* Are Press1993

Grof, Stanislav, M.D., Ph.D. *When The Impossible Happens* Sounds True 2006

Haisch, Bernard, *Journal of Scientific Exploration* Volume 7, Number 3, 1993

Heartung, A. Personal Interview Seattle, WA 2001

Jacquin , Linda, Personal Interview Seattle, WA 2001

Kardec, Allen, Blackwell, Anna *The Spirits Book* Brotherhood of Life 1989

Kircher P. M.D. Personal Interview Seattle, WA 2001

Kubler-Ross, Elisabeth, Blessing *in Disguise: Another Side of the Near-Death* 1997

Lagrand, Louis E. *After-Death Communication* Llewellyn Publications 1999

Lampham, Lewis, H. *Lapham's Quarterly* Volume VI, Number 4, 2013

Long, Jeff & Jodie, Personal Interviews Seattle, WA 2001

McKenna, Terence, *The Invisible Landscape* Seabury Press 1975

Moody, Jr. Raymond, A. M.D. *Life After Life* Bantam Books 1975

Moore, Thomas, *Care of Soul* Harper Collins 1992

Hallett, Elizbeath, www.Light-Hearts.com 2014

Monroe, Robert, A. *Ultimate Journey* Random House 1994

Morse, Melvin, M.D. Personal Interview Seattle, WA 2001

Musgrove. C. Personal Interview, 2000 Seattle, WA 2001

Newton, Michael Ph.D Personal Interview, Sacramento, CA 2003

Newton, Michael Ph.D *Destiny of Souls* Llewellyn Publications 2000

Newton, Michael Ph.D *Journey of Souls* Llewellyn Publications1994

Osis, Karlos, Ph.D., Haraldsson, Erlendur Ph.D. *At the Hour of Death* Avon 1977

Parnia et all, Resuscitation, Oct. 2014

Ring, Kenneth Ph.D., Cooper, Sharon *MindSight* William James Center for Consciousness Studies 1999

Ring, Kenneth, Ph.D. *Heading Toward Omega* Quill/William Morrow 1984

Ring, Kenneth, Ph.D. Valarino, Evelyn, E. *Lessons from the Light* Insight Books 1998

Ritchie, Teresa, Personal Interview Seattle, WA 2001

Salisbury, Edward, Personal Interview Seattle, WA 2001

Sharp, Clark, Kimberly, RN *After The Light* William Morrow 1995

Strassman, Rick, M.D. *DMT: The Sprit Molecule* Park Street Press 2001

Taylor, Bill, Personal Interview Seattle, WA 2001

Tompkins, Ptolemy, *The Modern Book of the Dead* Atria Books 2012

Thurman, Robert A.F. Translator, *The Tibetan Book of the Dead* 1994

Weiss, Brian, L. M.D. *Many Lives Manny Masters* Fireside Books 1988

Wimmer, Gary, L. *A Second in Eternity* 2012

Williams, Kevin, www.near-death.com 2014